Punitive Damages in Financial Injury Jury Verdicts

T0124055

Erik Moller

Nicholas M. Pace

Stephen J. Carroll

RAND

The Institute for Civil Justice

THE INSTITUTE FOR CIVIL JUSTICE

The mission of the Institute for Civil Justice is to help make the civil justice system more efficient and more equitable by supplying policymakers and the public with the results of objective, empirically based, analytic research. The ICJ facilitates change in the civil justice system by analyzing trends and outcomes, identifying and evaluating policy options, and bringing together representatives of different interests to debate alternative solutions to policy problems. The Institute builds on a long tradition of RAND research characterized by an interdisciplinary, empirical approach to public policy issues and rigorous standards of quality, objectivity, and independence.

ICJ research is supported by pooled grants from corporations, trade and professional associations, and individuals; by government grants and contracts; and by private foundations. The Institute disseminates its work widely to the legal, business, and research communities, and to the general public. In accordance with RAND policy, all Institute research products are subject to peer review before publication. ICJ publications do not necessarily reflect the opinions or policies of the research sponsors or of the ICJ Board of Overseers.

BOARD OF OVERSEERS

PREFACE

Studies of civil jury verdicts have been a prominent feature of the Institute for Civil Justice's research agenda since its inception. This work has included the creation of a database for the analysis of jury verdicts and descriptive and analytic studies of verdict trends.

Our current research extends our jury verdict work in two significant directions: First, it provides additional detail about punitive damage awards in cases in our existing database in which the plaintiff complains of financial injuries--cases in which punitive damages are awarded relatively more frequently than in other types of cases. Second, the database has been extended to include verdicts reached in Alabama from 1992 to 1997.

This study should be of interest to organizations, attorneys, and policymakers concerned with trends in civil justice and with civil justice reform. In light of the diversity of these audiences, we present our study results in two forms. This volume provides the details of our analysis and methods. A summary of our findings is contained in Erik Moller, Nicholas M. Pace, and Stephen J. Carroll, *Punitive Damages in Financial Injury Jury Verdicts: Executive Summary*, MR-889-ICJ, 1997.

For more information about the Institute for Civil Justice contact:

Dr. Deborah Hensler, Director
Institute for Civil Justice
RAND
1700 Main Street, P.O. Box 2138
Santa Monica, CA 90407-2138
TEL: (310)451-6916
FAX: (310)451-6979
Internet: Deborah_Hensler@rand.org

A profile of the ICJ, abstracts of its publications, and ordering information can be found on RAND's home page on the World Wide Web at http://www.rand.org/centers/icj.

CONTENTS

FIGURES

TABLES

SUMMARY

BACKGROUND

Punitive damages lie at the heart of the controversy about the
civil justice system and have been the focus of reform efforts at both
state and local levels of government. Many argue that punitive damages
have become an unpredictable feature of the legal landscape, imposing
burdens on business that are out of proportion to the alleged wrong-
doing. Others counter that punitive damages are necessary to punish and
deter egregious behavior and that amounts awarded are reasonably related
to corporate behavior.

Previous research conducted by the Institute for Civil Justice
(ICJ), based on jury verdicts from 1985 to 1994 in 15 jurisdictions
across the country, documented that, in general, punitive damages are
rare events. They are awarded in less than 4 percent of all verdicts;
however, the average punitive award amount was more than $1 million in
many of the jurisdictions examined (Moller, 1996).

This earlier research also established that within certain case
types, punitive damages occur relatively more often. In particular,
almost half of all punitive awards were made in cases in which the
damages were financial, rather than personal in nature. These verdicts,
which we call *financial injury verdicts* to distinguish them from
personal injury verdicts, comprise disputes arising from contractual or
commercial relationships including, for example, disputes arising from
insurance or employment contracts or from unfair business practices.

Little detailed information has been available about *financial
injury* cases. To provide an empirical basis for the ongoing debate
about punitive damages, we draw on the ICJ's jury verdict database to
describe the number of punitive damage awards in financial injury cases
in selected jurisdictions during the period 1985 to 1994 and to examine
patterns in these awards. We provide a separate analysis of jury
verdicts reached from 1992 to 1997 from all of Alabama. Because caps on
punitive damages are a prominent feature of many reform proposals, we

also estimate what percentage of the financial injury punitive awards in our database would have been affected by caps of various sizes and how the caps would have affected the total amount of punitive damages awarded in such cases.

THE DETERRENT AND SHADOW EFFECTS OF PUNITIVE DAMAGES

Most civil disputes are resolved by the parties without recourse to a lawsuit, and most of the civil cases in which a lawsuit is filed never reach a jury. However, even though they are rare, jury verdicts are important. Juries decide cases totaling billions of dollars annually. But the dollars that are awarded by juries are only one aspect of the influence of jury verdicts. Although the award is important to the parties in a case, the signals that awards send to the rest of society may have a far greater influence on our nation's social and economic well being.

Jury verdicts have both a deterrent and a shadow effect. The jury's decision in any particular case indicates the potential costs of engaging in behaviors similar to the defendant's. Jury verdicts thus set standards that can influence behavior and, by deterring unduly risky behavior, affect the financial and personal risks we impose on each other. At the same time, the jury's decision in any particular case indicates the potential outcome of any similar dispute. Jury verdicts thus cast shadows that influence claiming and settlement behavior, ultimately affecting the mix of cases that future juries will see and, coming full circle, the outcomes and precedents that will guide system participants in the future.

Legal theorists have observed that awards of compensatory damages have both deterrent and shadow effects. In principle, individuals and organizations involved in activities that can result in harm can learn from their own experiences and from those of other similarly situated parties, both the likelihood that they will be found liable for someone's losses and the likely size of those losses. They can adjust their behavior with a view toward the expected cost should someone claim that they are liable for harm. And, if a claim is brought, those expectations provide the parties a basis for negotiating a reasonable settlement.

But the deterrent and shadow effects of punitive damage awards may be far stronger and, thus, more significant, than the corresponding effects of compensatory awards. Punitive damages are designed to punish a defendant for grossly inappropriate actions and, in so doing, to deter future such actions by signaling that their consequences can be severe. Because punitive damages are awarded in a fraction of all verdicts, they are less frequent, and thus less predictable, than compensatory awards. And, because punitive damages can be many times the compensatory award (though some states have imposed limits on punitive damages in some types of cases), their size is less predictable. Individuals and organizations may find it more difficult to develop expectations as to both the kinds of behaviors that will result in a punitive award and the amount of any such award.

The effects of punitive awards on individuals' and organizations' behaviors will depend on how they weigh the uncertainties of a punitive award. Critics of the current system, for example, argue that the risk of a very large punitive award sometimes drives defendants to settle cases in which they believe the claim is not meritorious, or to settle meritorious claims for far too much.

How are business decisionmakers and litigants likely to respond to the risks of punitive damage awards? The literature on risk perception and management in business decisionmaking suggests that in assessing risks, most business decisionmakers focus on *worst-case scenarios* and will go to great lengths to avoid exposing their companies to very large financial losses or potential bankruptcy (March and Shapira, 1987)

Previous ICJ work (Garber, 1993) emphasizes that the nature of the worst-case scenario differs across industries. For example, for medical products, mass torts are very salient, and companies could be liable for punitive damages in many different cases. In contrast, in the automobile industry, the worst-case scenario might involve adverse publicity triggered by punitive damage awards, consequent loss of sales and company reputation, and responses of safety regulators. Punitive awards are important from this perspective because the presence of a punitive award increases the likelihood that newspapers and other media will report on a verdict and trigger such adverse publicity (Garber, work in progress).

Because there are differing perspectives about which features of punitive damage awards are most likely to influence decisionmakers and litigants, we report multiple measures of punitive damage awards. The mean award may be important because it is, in a statistical sense, the amount a defendant could expect to pay if a jury made a punitive award. The median award is important because the odds are exactly equal that a given punitive award will be greater than or less than the median punitive award. The 90th percentile award captures the worst-case scenario.

THE DATA USED IN THIS STUDY

The ICJ's jury verdict studies are supported by a unique jury verdict database constructed by the Institute over the past 15 years. This study focuses on data collected from 1985 to 1994 in jurisdictions constituting a diverse sample of geographical locations, population, growth, and income. The jurisdictions include all state trial courts of general jurisdiction in the states of California and New York; Cook County, Illinois (Chicago); the St. Louis, Missouri, metropolitan area; and Harris County, Texas (Houston).[1] The states in which these jurisdictions lie differ on important legal standards relevant to punitive damage awards, including limits on punitive awards, specification of the type of behavior that can warrant a punitive award, and different burdens of proof that must be met for a punitive award to be made. Variation in laws between states may explain some of the variation in jury verdict outcomes that we observe.

For all financial injury verdicts in which punitive damages were awarded, we identified the particular type of dispute that led to the punitive damage award and added information about the parties, their

---

[1]We omitted one very large financial injury verdict from Harris County—an award of more than $13 billion dollars, more than $3 billion of which was punitive—because it would have strongly affected many descriptions of the data. The next largest verdict in our database was less than one-thirtieth the size of this verdict.

relationship to each other, and the industrial sector in which the dispute arose.

We supplement data from these jurisdictions with information obtained from the Administrative Office of the Alabama Courts for verdicts reached in that state's trial courts of general jurisdiction during the period 1992 to 1997. Because these data differ in important ways from the data in the ICJ database, we report the Alabama data separately.

Overall, about one-quarter of the U.S. population (1995) lives in the jurisdictions included in this study.

It is important to keep the following facts in mind when interpreting jury verdict data:

- Cases tried to verdict may not be representative of all claims filed. Many claims are settled before reaching trial.
- The pattern of civil jury outcomes in any year or jurisdiction reflects the mix of cases tried to verdict in that year or jurisdiction, as well as jury decisions. The mix of cases may reflect changes in court jurisdiction, legal rules, and system user behavior.
- A substantial fraction of jury awards are reduced after verdict by trial or appellate court action or by settlement.
- We cannot assume that the patterns observed in one jurisdiction will be replicated in any other specific jurisdiction.

For all these reasons, jury verdict data are probably a more useful indicator of the signals that attorneys and potential claimants receive from the civil justice system than of the underlying dynamics of jury behavior.

PUNITIVE DAMAGE AWARDS IN FINANCIAL INJURY VERDICTS IN CALIFORNIA, COOK COUNTY, HARRIS COUNTY, THE ST. LOUIS METROPOLITAN AREA, AND NEW YORK: 1985 TO 1994

To put our discussion of financial injury verdicts in perspective, we first analyzed punitive awards in all verdicts in California; Cook County, Illinois; Harris County, Texas; metropolitan St. Louis; and New

York. We found patterns of punitive damages similar to those that emerged in our prior studies. Of the approximately 1,300 punitive damage verdicts in the database, about 50 percent occurred in financial injury verdicts.

To describe trends in financial injury punitive damage awards, we used the following descriptive measures:

- The number of punitive damage awards, the percentage of all verdicts (including defense and plaintiff victories) in which punitive damages were awarded, and the proportion of the total amount of damages awarded in all cases that was punitive.

- The punitive award amount: The mean award (arithmetic average) and the median award (typical award because half the award amounts lie above and half below it) to provide measures of central tendency, and the 90th percentile (10 percent of the awards lie above this amount) to provide information regarding extremely high award amounts.[2]

- The relationship between amount of compensatory damages and amount of punitive damages because the policy debate often focuses on this relationship. We calculate the ratio of punitive damages to compensatory damages for each case. A ratio of 1.0 means that punitive and compensatory damages were equal for that case. A ratio of greater than 1.0 means that punitive damages were higher than compensatory damages for that case. A ratio less than 1.0 means that punitive damages were lower than compensatory damages for that case. We focus on the median of the distribution of all these ratios.

VARIATION IN FINANCIAL INJURY PUNITIVE DAMAGE AWARDS BETWEEN MAJOR TYPES OF DISPUTES

To link our analysis more closely to the policy debate over punitive damages, we categorized the financial injury cases in our

---

[2]To control for inflation, we converted all award amounts to 1992 dollars.

database to reflect case types frequently mentioned in that debate. The
categories we used in our analysis are shown in Table S.1.

Table S.1
Types of Disputes in Our Sample

Types of Dispute	Definition
Insurance	Disputes involving the existence, interpretation, or performance of an insurance contract.
Employment	Disputes arising out of an employee-employer relationship.
Securities	Disputes arising out of the existence of a security instrument, including stocks, bonds, and other instruments of finance or ownership. Includes shareholder derivative suits.
Real property	Disputes arising out of the sale, lease, or improvement of real property.
Other contract	An aggregate of many types of contractual disputes other than those identified above.
Other commercial	Financial injury cases arising out of noncontractual relationships between the parties. Largely antitrust and unfair business practice.

As Table S.2 shows, in the jurisdictions we analyzed, punitive
damages were awarded in 14 percent of all financial injury verdicts.
Most of the punitive awards occurred in insurance, employment, and real
property disputes.

Punitive damage award amounts were often high in these cases. The
mean punitive awards varied from $2.1 million to $7.9 million, with an
overall mean of $5.2 million. (We exclude *securities* and *other
commercial* cases because we have so few data points.) The overall 90th
percentile award amount was $6.2 million.

Given these large award amounts, it is not surprising that punitive
damages represent a large portion of the total amount of damages awarded
in these case types. As Figure S.1 shows, punitive damages represent
more than half of all the damages awarded overall, including those cases
in which there was no punitive award and more than 60 percent in
insurance and securities cases.

Table S.2

**Variation in Punitive Awards in Financial Injury Case Types
(1985 to 1994)**

Type of Dispute	No. of Punitive Awards	Punitive Awards as % of No. of Verdicts	Damage Awards ($1992)		
			Mean	Median	90th Percentile
Insurance	134	13	7,933,676	652,000	13,572,000
Employment	125	17	2,689,033	194,180	2,060,200
Securities	6	21	30,269,389	1,229,080	174,342,000
Real property	113	12	2,110,888	94,700	2,048,000
Other contracts	258	15	6,283,804	277,875	8,423,360
Other commercial	11	36	1,654,966	956,470	3,370,840
Overall	647	14	5,344,876	250,000	6,223,400

Because there are so few cases in the *securities* and *other commercial* categories, we do not believe statistics for these case types necessarily reflect cases not in our database.

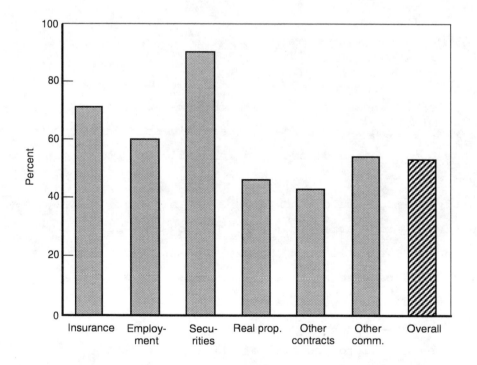

**Figure S.1—Punitive Damages as a Percentage of
Total Award Amount**

The relationship between the amount of punitive and compensatory damages awarded in any given case has been prominent in the policy debate, and some federal and state judiciaries and legislatures use the amount of compensatory damages awarded as one factor in judging the reasonableness of the punitive award. We use the ratio of punitive damages to compensatory damages for each case to explore the relative size of punitive damage award amounts for these case types.

Figure S.2 shows the median of this ratio for each type. The highest median ratio is found in insurance verdicts, where punitive awards are almost four times compensatory awards. The overall median ratio is 1.4.

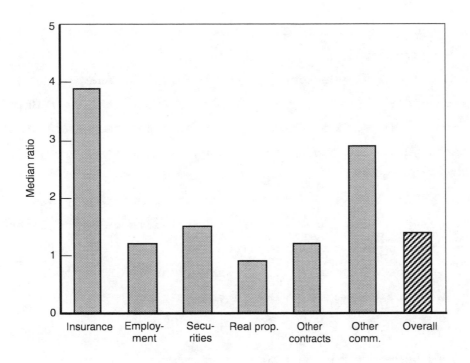

Figure S.2—Median Ratio of Punitive Award to Compensatory Award

VARIATION IN PUNITIVE AWARDS BETWEEN JURISDICTIONS

As Table S.3 shows, punitive damages are awarded more often in California and Harris County than in the other jurisdictions in our database. Punitive damages are awarded in about 20 percent of all

Table S.3

Variation in Punitive Awards In Financial Injury Case Types
Between Jurisdictions (1985 To 1994)

Jurisdiction	No. of Punitive Awards	Punitive Awards as % of No. of Verdicts	Damage Awards ($1992)		
			Mean	Median	90th Percentile
California	429	21	5,844,685	355,800	7,210,700
Cook County	17	4	3,233,558	250,000	3,000,000
Harris County	130	14	6,669,497	206,314	8,335,000
St. Louis Metro. area	55	7	357,229	37,050	592,800
New York	16	4	567,579	55,127	3,755,500
Overall	647	14	5,344,876	250,000	6,223,400

financial injury verdicts in California and in 14 percent of all
financial injury verdicts in Harris County.

Award amounts vary across jurisdictions. The mean punitive damage
award is considerably higher in California, Cook County, or Harris
County than in New York or the St. Louis metropolitan area. And in the
former three jurisdictions, punitive damages represent more than half of
total damages awarded.

Although the ratio of punitive award to compensatory award also
varies across jurisdictions, the pattern of variance is different (Fig.
S.3). The St. Louis metropolitan area, which has the lowest median,
mean, and 90th percentile punitive awards, has a higher median ratio of
punitive award to compensatory award than either California or Harris
County.

VARIATION IN PUNITIVE DAMAGE AWARDS OVER TIME

We examined the entire population of financial injury verdicts in
our database for each of the five-year periods 1985-1989 and 1990-1994.
The number of punitive awards has decreased between these periods, both
in absolute numbers and as a percentage of the overall number of
verdicts. Punitive damages were awarded in about 16 percent of all
financial injury verdicts in the 1985-1989 period and in about 13
percent of all financial injury verdicts in the 1990-1994 period. This
change reflects the facts that plaintiffs are winning at a slightly

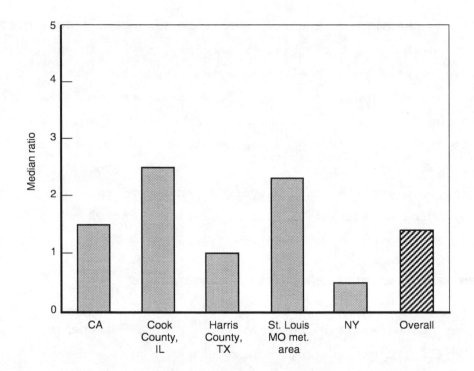

Figure S.3—Median Ratio of Punitive Award to Compensatory Award in Different Jurisdictions

lower rate, and given that they have won the case, plaintiffs are also being awarded punitive damages at a slightly lower rate as well.[3]

However, the mean award amount increased from $3.4 million to $7.6 million between these two periods. In addition, punitive damages represent a larger portion of all damages awarded, rising from about 44 percent of all damages awarded in the 1985-1989 period to slightly less than 60 percent of all damages awarded in the 1990-1994 period.

In contrast, the median ratio of punitive damages to compensatory damages fell over the two periods from 1.5 to 1.2, indicating that there is an increase in the number of punitive damage awards in which the amount of punitive damages awarded is small relative to the compensatory damages awarded.

---

[3]The question of whether these changes reflect changed jury behavior or changes in plaintiffs' and defendants' litigation strategies, which, in turn, changed the mix of cases going to verdict, is beyond the scope of this analysis.

MORE DETAILED ANALYSES OF PUNITIVE AWARDS IN FINANCIAL INJURY CASES

In the technical volume that is a companion to this executive summary, we provide more detailed analyses of punitive awards in financial injury cases. In particular, we describe trends in punitive awards in the four types of financial injury cases in which these awards occur most frequently—insurance, employment, real property, and other contracts. We examine patterns in punitive awards according to the legal theory employed in these disputes. And we compare differences in awards depending on whether the plaintiff was an individual or a government, business, or other entity.

ESTIMATED EFFECT OF CAPS ON PUNITIVE DAMAGE AWARDS

Many states have already approved caps on punitive damage awards, and similar measures are being considered in other states and at the federal level. To provide some context for the policy debate, we estimated what the effects would have been of imposing caps on the existing financial injury punitive awards in our database from California, Cook County, Harris County, metropolitan St. Louis, and New York.[4]

The caps we analyzed are different multiples of the compensatory damages awarded in the case. We chose multiples of one through five and ten—an array of proposals that spans legislative efforts in many states.

If punitive damages had been capped at the amount of compensatory damages in each case, 60 percent of all punitive awards would have been affected, and the total amount of punitive damages awarded in these cases would have been reduced by roughly 65 percent. If caps had been imposed at higher levels, fewer awards and a smaller percentage of the damages awarded would have been affected. For example, a cap of three times compensatory damages would have affected the punitive damage award in about one-third of all the financial injury punitive awards and decreased the total amount of punitive damages awarded by 40 percent.

_____

[4]Since 1987, Harris County has capped punitive damages at the greater of four times compensatory damages or $200,000 except in cases of malice or intentional tort. Consequently, for Harris County our estimate is the effect of imposing caps beyond the cap already in place.

Table S.4 displays our estimates of the effects of caps on the punitive damage awards in our database.

Were such caps to be imposed, the future experience in the states in our database would not necessarily reflect these estimates. Legislation imposing caps would also affect claiming and settlement behavior. In addition, if juries were aware of caps, they might take limits on punitive damages into their calculations of compensatory damages.

Table S.4
Effect of Caps on Punitive Damages in Financial Injury Verdicts

Level of Limit (multiples of compensatory damages)	No. of Punitive Awards Affected	% of Punitive Awards Affected	Decrease of Aggregate Total Award (%)	Decrease of Aggregate Punitive Award (%)
1	386	60	43	66
2	280	43	34	51
3	219	34	27	40
4	184	28	22	33
5	168	26	19	27
10	102	16	10	12

PUNITIVE DAMAGE AWARDS IN ALABAMA: 1992 TO 1997

The incidence and size of punitive damage awards in Alabama has figured prominently in the national debate over punitive damages, but heretofore little systematic information has been available about such awards in that state. We analyzed data describing verdicts reached in Alabama's trial courts of general jurisdiction from 1992 to 1997.

We estimate that the percentage of all financial injury verdicts in which punitive damages were awarded in Alabama is between 17 and 32 percent during the period 1992 to 1997.[5] To put this range in perspective,

---

[5]We present our results for Alabama as a range because some "general awards" are reported as a lump sum, without distinguishing what portion, if any, is a punitive award. The lower number in our estimated range of 17 to 32 percent assumes that the awards are entirely compensatory; the upper number assumes that they are entirely punitive.

in the other jurisdictions we found a low of 4 percent (in New York) and a high of 21 percent (in California). In Alabama, punitive damages represented between 80 and 86 percent of all damages awarded in all financial injury verdicts.

As with the other states in our database, punitive damage awards in Alabama can be quite high. The mean punitive damage award is between $540,000 and $945,000; the 90th percentile award is between $947,000 and $1.9 million.

The median ratio of punitive damages to compensatory damages in Alabama is somewhat over 5; this compares to 0.5 to 2.5 in the other jurisdictions studied. These data suggest that in Alabama punitive damages are awarded more often and are higher in any given case relative to compensatory damages than in the other jurisdictions in our database.

We also estimated the effects of a range of caps on punitive damage awards in the Alabama data.[6] Because we cannot determine how this statute affects litigant and jury behavior, our estimates must be read with caution.

We estimate that a cap at the level of compensatory damages would have affected approximately 80 percent of the punitive awards in Alabama and would have reduced the total amount of punitive damages awarded by about 90 percent. A cap at three times compensatory damages would have affected the punitive damages awarded in 60 percent of the punitive damage awards in financial injury cases in Alabama and reduced the total amount of punitive damages awarded in these cases by 82 percent. In our estimates, we assumed that all general awards were compensatory. Had we assumed that they were in part or entirely punitive in nature, the effect of caps would have been larger.

---

[6]Alabama law limits punitive damages to $250,000, unless the defendant has exhibited a pattern or practice of intentional wrongful conduct involving actual malice or libel, slander or defamation.

ACKNOWLEDGMENTS

The authors are indebted to the many people who have contributed to the preparation of this report. We thank the jury verdict reporters who provided the data for this study; the Survey Research Group Staff who collected the information; Patricia Bedrosian for her editorial and production assistance; Mary Vaiana for helping us to clarify our discussion; Jim Kakalik, Lloyd Dixon, and Deborah Hensler for their thoughtful comments; and the American Council of Life Insurance for their support.

1. INTRODUCTION

Jury verdicts have played a prominent role in the current tort reform debate. Proponents of tort reform cite high-profile jury verdicts as proof that the system is out of control--allegedly overcompensating plaintiffs, inappropriately harming defendants, and imposing unnecessary costs on the U.S. economy. In addition, these critics argue, the civil justice system currently places a heavy administrative burden on the courts by encouraging frivolous claims which in turn divert limited court resources from legitimate claims.

On the other hand, opponents of these reform efforts argue that reforms will prevent legitimate claims from being pursued, thus denying individuals redress for harm resulting from egregious behavior. Furthermore, these reforms will eliminate important incentives to avoid such behavior in the future.

Reform efforts at both the state and federal levels seek to limit, directly and indirectly, the amount of damages that can be awarded. Limiting joint and several liability, capping punitive damages in some or all cases, and imposing limits on damages in medical malpractice cases directly affect jury verdicts. These and other reforms, such as limiting attorneys' fees, would also indirectly affect jury verdicts by influencing which cases attorneys take, and, therefore, which cases juries decide.

Of all the issues on the tort reform agenda, issues surrounding punitive damages have probably attracted the most vigorous debate. Many argue that punitive damages have become an unpredictable feature of the legal landscape, imposing considerable burdens on business. However, others counter that punitive damages are necessary to punish and deter egregious behavior.

Previous ICJ research has established that, in general, punitive damages are infrequently awarded. However, within certain case types, punitive damages are awarded much more frequently than in other case types. In particular, cases in which the injuries suffered by the plaintiff are financial in nature receive punitive damage awards much more frequently than cases in which the injuries suffered by the plaintiff are personal in nature.[1] Cases in which the injuries suffered by the plaintiff are financial in nature include, for example, disputes over insurance or employment contracts or disputes arising out of unfair business practices. These verdicts do not involve other familiar civil causes of action, such as automobile personal injury, product liability, or medical malpractice. In this report, we call these cases "financial injury verdicts" to distinguish them from "personal injury verdicts."

There are no sharp distinctions in the law when it comes to dividing actions brought in the civil courts into case type categories, especially when using the injuries or losses suffered by the plaintiff as the key. For example, personal injury cases almost always involve requests for economic damages in the form of medical bills, rehabilitation costs, loss of wages and future earnings, and property damage. On the other hand, many "financial injury" cases contain elements of physical harm to the plaintiff in that severe mental distress is alleged to result from the breach of a contract or failure to honor a claim. We identify financial injury cases as those in which the litigation concerns damages that arise directly from the breach of contract, the fraudulent embezzlement of the partnership's assets, the wrongful termination of employment, etc. The concept of "financial injuries" is not a new one; past ICJ research has used the term "business cases" to capture the exact same types of litigation (to some, the term "business" case implies that actual businesses are involved and, we will see, many financial injuries are brought for and against individuals).

Unfortunately, relatively little information has been previously available about financial injury verdicts. To provide an empirical basis for the ongoing policy debate about punitive damages, we draw on the jury verdict database constructed by the Institute for Civil Justice (ICJ) at RAND. We describe the number of punitive damages awarded in financial injury verdicts in selected jurisdictions during the period 1985 to 1994 and examine patterns in these awards. We have recently

---

[1]Personal injury verdicts include injuries to person and to property.

supplemented this database with information on jury verdicts in Alabama from approximately 1992 to 1997 and add a description of these data to our analysis.

In the next section, we provide background for our discussion by suggesting how jury verdicts, and punitive awards, influence participants in the civil justice system and by describing our approach in this study. In Section 3, we provide descriptive data about punitive damage awards in financial injury cases from 1985 to 1994 in California, Cook County, Illinois, Harris County, Texas, St. Louis metropolitan area, Missouri, and New York. In Section 4, we describe our initial analysis of punitive damages awards in Alabama from 1992-1997.[2] Last, we summarize the important findings and conclusions from this research.

_____

[2]We describe these data separately because they are collected using very different methods and from different time periods. As such, they are generally incomparable with our data from other states.

2. BACKGROUND AND APPROACH

WHY CARE ABOUT JURY VERDICTS?

Although high-profile jury verdicts have become lightning rods in the reform debate, most cases never reach juries. The vast majority of disputes are resolved by negotiated settlement, abandonment, or rulings at an earlier stage of the litigation. One recent study estimated that the percentage of complaints filed that reach a jury verdict is 1.6 percent.[1] In many jurisdictions, the number of cases actually reaching a jury verdict has been falling over the last 10 years (Moller, 1996). Plaintiffs win a fraction of these cases, and only a fraction of these plaintiff victories result in a punitive damage award. Given the relative infrequency of both jury verdicts and punitive damages, should we care about them? The answer is yes, for several reasons.

Juries resolve tens of thousands of disputes nationwide every year,[2] deciding cases totaling billions of dollars. And jury decisions establish standards that influence the behavior of our society. Equally important, jury verdicts influence the behavior of users of the civil justice system.

Juries make decisions that influence the civil justice system in two ways. First, juries determine whether the plaintiff wins, and if so, how much the plaintiff will be awarded, thus establishing guidelines that will be used to value future disputes. Second, in a small fraction of cases, verdicts are appealed to higher courts, creating precedent regarding substantive and procedural rules binding on future lawsuits.

Both outcomes and precedents influence the behavior of users of the system by establishing signals as to what other juries might do.

---

[1] See DeFrances, C., et al., *Civil Jury Cases and Verdicts in Large Counties*, Bureau of Justice Statistics, NCJ-154346 (1995).

[2] The Department of Justice, Bureau of Justice Statistics, estimates that juries in the state courts of general jurisdiction in the nation's largest 75 counties decided approximately 12,000 cases in the year ending June 30, 1992. DeFrances, C., et al., *Civil Jury Cases and Verdicts in Large Counties*, Bureau of Justice Statistics, NCJ-154346 (1995).

Attorneys, litigants, and potential litigants use these signals to evaluate disputes. Changes in these signals will affect the incentives and decisions of attorneys, litigants, and potential litigants to bring suit or to settle once suit has begun. In addition, business decisionmakers consider jury verdicts in determining the costs and benefits of various business decisions.[3] In this regard, jury verdicts provide important signals about the cost of business decisionmaking in our society.

In turn, the claiming and settlement behaviors of the system's users affect the mix of cases tried to the jury.[4] It is from this mix of cases that juries create the outcomes and precedents that guide system participants in the future.

THE SHADOW AND DETERRENT EFFECT OF PUNITIVE DAMAGES

Punitive damages play a critical and controversial role in this process. Critics argue that inappropriate punitive damage awards provide decisionmakers and litigants with incentives to engage in socially harmful behavior, such as removing useful products from the market and underinvesting in innovation. Proponents counter that punitive damage awards appropriately punish egregious behavior and provide the necessary incentives to prevent future harmful acts.

The effect of punitive damages on business decisionmaking and the civil justice process differs from that of compensatory jury verdicts. Unlike other jury awards, punitive damages are not designed to compensate for injuries that have been incurred. Rather, they are designed to punish a defendant for inappropriate actions described

---

[3]This effect has been termed the "jury's shadow." See Mnookin, R., and L. Kornhauser, "Bargaining in the Shadow of the Law: The Case of Divorce," *Yale Law Journal*, Vol. 88, No. 5, April 1979, pp. 980-57; Galanter, M., "The Regulatory Function of the Civil Jury," in Litan, R., ed., *Verdict: Assessing the Civil Jury System*, Washington, D.C.: The Brookings Institution, 1993, pp. 61-102. Understanding trends in jury verdicts is necessary to understanding this shadow.

[4]Of course, litigant behavior is also affected by many factors other than jury verdicts--for example, appellate decisions, administrative rulings, and other explanations of legal standards and rules. In addition, behavior will be affected by litigation strategy, legal cost estimates, public relations, and other factors not related to estimates of the legal standards.

variously, in different states, as malicious, oppressive, fraudulent, grossly negligent, or wanton and reckless.[5] In theory, punitive damages should deter such future actions by signaling that their consequences can be severe. In some states, the size of punitive damages is loosely linked to the size of the compensatory damages awarded;[6] in other states, punitive damages are not limited. Punitive damages can be many times the compensatory award, and, in the consumer context, can be imposed in multiple suits arising out of a single course of defendant behavior. These characteristics, in particular the uncertainty that punitive damages create, have caused many to argue that the threat of punitive damages provides strong incentive to defendants in suits that could involve punitive damages to settle cases in which the defendant believes the plaintiff's claims are non-meritorious or inflated because of the risk of a large punitive damage award.

What features of punitive damage awards are most likely to influence decisionmakers and litigants? Do they focus on the likelihood of such award--typically modest--or do they focus on the amounts awarded, however rare their occurrence? The literature on risk perception and management in business decisionmaking--which is not focused on punitive damages or liability costs--suggests that in assessing risks, most business decisionmakers focus on worst-case scenarios, and they will go to great lengths to avoid exposing their companies to potential disaster such as financial losses that are large in relation to the size of the company and, especially, bankruptcy (March and Shapira, 1987).

---

[5]Compensatory damages arguably provide both a compensatory mechanism for plaintiffs and a deterrent mechanism for defendants. However, some legal scholars argue that compensatory damages force defendants to internalize costs that they will pass on in the price of their goods. (Calebresi 1970), (Posner 1986), (Hirsch 1979), and (Shavell 1987).

[6]A number of states have limited punitive damages to various multiples of compensatory damages, and others are considering such legislation. See, e.g., Colorado--Colo. Rev. Stat. §§ 13-21-102(1)(a) and (3) (1987) (caps punitive damages at amount of actual damages), Connecticut--Conn. Gen. Stat. § 52-240b (1995) (caps punitive damages at twice compensatory damages in products liability cases), and Florida--Fla. Stat. §§ 768.73(1)(a) and (b) (Supp. 1992) (caps punitive damages at three times compensatory damages).

Our previous work applies these findings in the context of product liability litigation costs in general and punitive damages in product liability litigation in particular. That work emphasizes that the nature of the "worst-case scenario"--and the role of punitive damages-- differs across industries. For example, for medical products, mass torts are very salient, and companies could be liable for punitive damages in many different cases. In this context, the largest plausible total of awards across cases would tend to weigh very heavily upon the decisionmakers' analysis. In contrast, in the automobile industry, the worst-case scenario might involve adverse publicity triggered by punitive damage awards, consequent loss of sales and company reputation, and responses of safety regulators. Punitive awards might be important from this perspective because the presence of a punitive award increases the likelihood that newspapers and other media will report on a verdict and trigger such adverse publicity (Garber, 1993). Our work in progress indicates that the presence of any punitive component to an award substantially increases the likelihood of newspaper coverage, even holding constant the total size of the award, which suggests that frequencies or probabilities of punitive damage awards could be very salient to decisionmakers (Garber, work in progress).

Additional measures of punitive awards are important from other perspectives. The mean award may be important because it is, in a statistical sense, the amount a defendant could expect to pay if a jury made a punitive award. The median award is important because the odds are exactly equal that a given punitive award will be greater than or less than the median punitive award.

Different decisionmakers in different industries may respond in different ways to these measures of punitive damage awards. In the discussion that follows, we report a variety of measures reflecting each of the potential perspectives on punitive awards.

PREVIOUS ICJ RESEARCH ON PUNITIVE DAMAGE AWARDS

Reflecting the import of jury verdicts in the civil justice system, the Institute for Civil Justice (ICJ) has been conducting research on jury verdicts since 1982, describing trends in verdicts and analyzing possible explanations for them. For example, ICJ research documented jurisdictional differences in jury verdicts (Shanley and Peterson, 1983), as well as increasing jury awards in the early-1980s in different jurisdictions (Peterson, 1987). Other studies showed that corporate defendants pay out more than individual defendants for similar injuries (Chin and Peterson, 1985), and that they were more likely to suffer a punitive damage award (Peterson, Sarma, and Shanley, 1987). Most recently ICJ research has described trends in civil jury verdicts from 1985 to 1994 (Moller, 1996).

These analyses are supported by a unique jury verdict database constructed by the ICJ over the past 15 years. The database consists of all civil jury verdicts reached in the courts of general jurisdiction[7] in San Francisco County, California, and Cook County, Illinois, from 1960 to 1994; in all other California counties from 1980 to 1994; and from four additional states[8] from 1985 to 1994.[9]

The data are collected from jury verdict reporters within these jurisdictions. Jury verdict reporters are private subscription newsletters for lawyers and litigants that report the outcomes and relevant information about jury verdicts in their respective jurisdictions.[10] In creating the ICJ database, we used two criteria to

---

[7]Data collected from 1960 to 1980 include decisions from both state and federal courts of general jurisdiction. Data collected from 1985 to 1994 are from the state courts of general jurisdiction only.

[8]The additional states included in the database are Missouri, New York, Texas, and Washington. The data include jury verdict information from the state courts of general jurisdiction in: 1) the St. Louis metropolitan area in Missouri; 2) all of New York; 3) Harris County, Texas (Houston); and 4) King County, Washington (Seattle).

[9]Previous ICJ studies reporting on these data include Peterson, M., and G. Priest, *The Civil Jury: Trends in Trials and Verdicts, Cook County, Illinois, 1960-1979*, Santa Monica, Calif.: RAND, R-2881-ICJ, 1982; Shanley, M., and M. Peterson, *Comparative Justice: Civil Jury Verdicts in San Francisco and Cook Counties, 1959-1980*, Santa Monica, Calif.: RAND, R-3006-ICJ, 1983; Peterson, M., *Civil Juries in the 1980s: Trends in Jury Trials and Verdicts in California and Cook County, Illinois*, Santa Monica, Calif.: RAND, R-3466-ICJ, 1987.

[10]For a more complete description of the methods used in collecting this data see: Peterson, M., and G. Priest, *The Civil Jury: Trends in Trials and Verdicts, Cook County, Illinois, 1960-1979*, Santa Monica, Calif.: RAND, R-2881-ICJ, 1982, Moller, E., *Trends in Civil Jury Verdicts since 1985*, Santa Monica, Calif.: RAND, MR-694-ICJ, 1996.

choose the jurisdictions--the existence of a reliable jury verdict reporter, and, given this restriction, geographic, jurisdictional, and socioeconomic diversity.[11] The jurisdictions we selected constitute a diverse sample in terms of geographical location, population, growth over the last ten years, race, and household income. The sample includes the three most populous counties in the nation: Los Angeles County, California; Cook County, Illinois; and Harris County, Texas, in order, as well as the fifth and sixth largest--Orange County, California; and Kings County, New York. It also includes urban, suburban, and rural counties. This diversity allows us to consider whether there is consistency in jury outcomes over time and across the country.

With the addition of Alabama, about 25 percent of the nation's population reside in jurisdictions in the ICJ jury verdict database.

We determined the reliability of the jury verdict reporter primarily by its method of data collection. Jury verdict reports that rely on attorneys to tell them about jury outcomes inevitably report a biased sample of jury verdicts. We consider a jury verdict reporter to be reliable if it uses its own staff to gather information about verdicts.

Despite the attention they have received from policymakers and the media, overall punitive damages are awarded infrequently. Previous ICJ research on jury verdicts from 1985 to 1994 in selected jurisdictions (Moller, 1996)[12] indicated that for these selected jurisdictions the overall percentage of verdicts in which punitive damages are awarded is less than 4 percent. This percentage varies between different

---

[11]Alabama does not have a statewide jury verdict reporter with a long-term history of publication. We rely on data provided by the Administrative Office of the Alabama Courts for this analysis of verdicts in that state and describe our findings in a separate chapter of this report.

[12]This research studied jury verdicts in fifteen jurisdictions from the ICJ database: Los Angeles County, Orange County, Sacramento County, and San Francisco County from California; Cook County from Illinois; Jefferson County, St. Charles County, St. Louis City, and St. Louis County from Missouri; Erie County, Kings County, Manhattan County, and Nassau County from New York, Harris County from Texas; and King County from Washington.

jurisdictions, ranging from 7 percent in Harris County, Texas (Houston), to less than 2 percent in Cook County, Illinois (Chicago) and New York County, New York (Manhattan).[13]

However, this research indicated that within these jurisdictions punitive damages are concentrated in certain case types. For example, most punitive damage awards occur in intentional tort cases[14] or financial injury cases;[15] 35 percent of all punitive damage awards occur in intentional tort cases and 47 percent occur in financial injury cases. No other cases type represents more than 10 percent of all punitive damage verdicts.

Moreover, in intentional tort and financial injury case types punitive damages likely play an important role. For example, punitive awards are made in 17 percent of all intentional tort cases and in 14 percent of all financial injury cases. By comparison, punitive damages are awarded in only 2.6 percent of all product liability verdicts.[16]

Within these jurisdictions, punitive damage award amounts are quite high--often the subject of high-profile media coverage. Punitive damage award amounts varied between case types. The highest punitive damage award--$3,912,000,000--occurred in a financial injury case in Harris County; the second highest punitive damage award--$375,187,800--occurred in a financial injury case in Los Angeles County.[17]

---

[13]This low percentage of punitive damage awards is consistent with other studies. See DeFrances, et al., *Civil Jury Cases and Verdicts in Large Counties*, Washington, D.C.: U.S. Department of Justice, 1995 p. 8.

[14]Intentional tort includes assault, battery, theft, harassment, libel, slander, and other actions where the defendant actually intended to harm the plaintiff. These disputes represent very different cases from those included in this analysis, and for that reason we are not including them in this report.

[15]Cases we describe as "financial injury" verdicts were referred to as "business verdicts" in our previous research. However, we felt that "business" is misleading because these verdicts include cases in which individual parties, not just business litigants, are involved.

[16]Moller, E., *Trends in Civil Jury Verdicts since 1985*, Santa Monica, Calif.: RAND, MR-694-ICJ, 1996. Again, these findings are confirmed by other research. See DeFrances, et al., *Civil Jury Cases and Verdicts in Large Counties*, Washington, D.C.: U.S. Department of Justice, 1995 p. 8.

[17]Moller, E., *Trends in Civil Jury Verdicts since 1985*, Santa Monica, Calif.: RAND, MR-694-ICJ, 1996.

FOCUS OF THIS STUDY

Our previous research highlighted financial injury cases as having more frequent punitive awards. But what kinds of financial injury cases? In all jurisdictions? Have the case types changed over time? However, the existing database did not provide sufficient detail to answer these questions. To investigate such questions, we supplemented our existing database with more descriptive information for the subpopulation of cases identified as financial injury cases.

For all financial injury verdicts in which punitive damages were awarded, we identified the particular type of dispute that led to the punitive damage award. We also added more information about the parties, their relationship to each other, and the industrial sector (including manufacturing, commercial, or service sectors) in which the dispute arose. To help us understand the effect of punitive damage awards within these case types, we gathered similar information for a sample of financial injury cases in which punitive damages were not awarded--for example, defense verdicts and compensatory damage only verdicts.[18] For this current research we are studying all jurisdictions from the ICJ jury verdict database for the period 1985 to 1994.[19]

Our database was also extended to include Alabama. Alabama has developed a reputation as having pro-plaintiff juries. To investigate whether Alabama jury outcomes are different from those in the other states in our database, we have obtained data from the Administrative Office of the Alabama Courts. Although these data are not as detailed as the information we have for the other jurisdictions in this analysis, they will allow us to compare Alabama in a general way with five other states in our database. We present the Alabama data in a separate section of this report since there exist significant differences between the years covered by these data and the collection methodology used to collect these data and that used to collect the data from the other remaining states in our database.

---

[18]See Appendix A for a more detailed description of the data collection methods employed.

[19]See Peterson, M., and G. Priest, *The Civil Jury: Trends in Trials and Verdicts, Cook County, Illinois, 1960-1979*, Santa Monica, Calif.: RAND, R-2881-ICJ, 1982.

Some punitive damage award amounts are very large. Extremely large award amounts strongly affect the descriptive statistics that we employ in this study. We have omitted one very large financial injury verdict from Houston--an award of over $13 billion dollars, over $3 billion of which was punitive in nature. The next largest verdict in our database was less than one-thirtieth the size of this verdict. Because it is such a large verdict, this award would have strongly affected many descriptions of the data.

INTERPRETING JURY VERDICT DATA

It is important to keep the following facts in mind when interpreting jury verdict data:

- Cases tried to verdict are not representative of all claims filed. Attorneys settle many cases either to avoid anticipated adverse awards or because the expected award does not justify additional litigation expense.

- The pattern of civil jury outcomes in any year--including determinations of defendant liability, award amount, and punitive damages--reflects the mix of cases tried to verdict that year, as well as jury decisions. In turn, the mix of cases reaching juries may reflect changes in user behavior regarding claiming and settlement behavior.

- In addition, legal substantive and procedural rules will affect user behavior. Therefore, differences in these rules could also affect the mix of cases reaching juries and the observed jury outcomes. The jurisdictions in this study differ on important legal standards relevant to the award of punitive damages. These rules include, for example, limits on punitive damages (in general or in some specific case types), different types of defendant behavior that can warrant a punitive award, and different burdens of proof that a plaintiff must meet to obtain a punitive award. Table 2.1 provides some examples of how these rules vary between the states represented in our database.[20] This list is not exhaustive and is provided to give some idea of the variation in legal rules between jurisdictions.

- A substantial percentage of jury awards are reduced after verdict by trial court or appellate court action or by settlement. Previous ICJ research (Shanley and Peterson, 1987) found that, on average, about 70 percent of dollars awarded were paid out. In cases where punitive damages were awarded, slightly less than 60 percent of the amount awarded was paid. The data in our database do not include post-trial adjustments to jury verdicts made by later rulings.

- The size of jury awards varies substantially across jurisdictions, and we do not know whether the trends observed in one jurisdiction reflect patterns in other areas.

Since jury verdict data provide information on outcomes of jury trials only and no data on other aspects of the civil justice process, they are a more useful indicator of the signals that attorneys and litigants receive from juries than they are of the underlying dynamics of jury behavior or of the other participants in the system.[21]

Other research methods are useful for describing the civil justice system. However, there are inevitable tradeoffs among the jury research methods. Archival research, such as this and other ICJ jury verdict studies, is the best method for describing trends in jury outcomes. Other methods (for example, jury simulation experiments or postverdict interviews) are better suited for explaining the dynamics of jury

---

[20]The state of Washington does not allow punitive damage awards. Therefore, although our database contains information from a jury verdict reporter in Washington, we have excluded Washington from this analysis.

[21]Priest, G., and B. Klein, "The Selection of Disputes for Litigation," *Journal of Legal Studies*, Vol. 13, No. 1, 1984, pp. 1-55, presents the seminal discussion of the relation between disputant decisionmaking and case mix.

behavior; however, these methods are inappropriate for describing the magnitude of and variation in actual jury verdicts.[22]

Our goal for this report is to describe better the effect of punitive damages within the financial injury subpopulation of cases in which punitive damages are prevalent. Throughout our discussion, our presentation is descriptive; we make no attempt to explain the patterns in verdicts that we observe.

---

[22] See MacCoun, R., "Inside the Black Box: What Empirical Research Tells Us about Decisionmaking by Civil Juries," in Litan, R., ed., *Verdict: Assessing the Civil Jury System*, Washington, D.C.: The Brookings Institution, 1993 pp. 137-80, for a good description of the relative benefits of jury research methods.

Table 2.1

Illustrative Differences in Punitive Damage Law in Study Jurisdictions[1]

	Alabama	California	Illinois	Missouri	New York	Texas
Standard of Conduct	"...the defendant consciously or deliberately engaged in oppression, fraud, wantonness, or malice with regard to the plaintiff."[2]	"...[prove that] the defendant has been guilty of oppression, fraud, or malice."[3]	Defendant must have acted with fraud, actual malice, and deliberate violence or oppression or acted willfully or with such gross negligence as to indicate a wanton disregard of the rights of others.[4]	Punitives authorized when the defendant's conduct was outrageous because of the defendant's evil motive or reckless indifference to the rights of others.[5]	Punitive damages recoverable upon proof of 1) actual malice or ill will, 2) a morally culpable wrong, or 3) a wrongful act done willfully, wantonly, or maliciously.[6]	Punitives awarded only upon proof of fraud, malice, or gross negligence.[7]
Standard of Proof	Clear and Convincing Evidence[8]	Clear and Convincing Evidence[9]	Preponderance only	Preponderance only[10]	Preponderance only[11]	Preponderance only[12]
Compensatory Damages Required to Support Punitive Award?	No[13]	Yes[14]	Yes[15]	Yes[16]	Yes[17]	Yes[18]
Limitations on Punitive Award Amounts	Punitives can not exceed $250,000 unless based upon either 1) a pattern or practice of intentional wrongful conduct, even though the damage or injury was inflicted only on the plaintiff; or 2) conduct involving actual malice other than fraud or bad faith not part of a pattern or practice; or, 3) libel, slander, or defamation.[19]	No Explicit Guidelines.[20]	No Explicit Guidelines.[21]	No Explicit Guidelines.[22]	No Explicit Guidelines.[23]	Except in cases of malice or intentional tort, punitive damages may not exceed the greater of four times the actual damages or $200,000.[24]
Purpose includes Compensation[25]						X[26]
Purpose includes Punishment	X	X	X	X	X	X
Purpose includes Deterrence of Defendant	X	X	X	X	X	X
Purpose includes Deterrence of Other	X	X	X	X	X	X

[1] This table is presented for illustrative purposes only and attempts to reflect the state of the law in early 1992. Case and statutory law in each of these jurisdictions underwent varying degrees of evolution over the periods represented by trials in our database. For example, the "Clear and Convincing" evidence standard was not instituted in California until 1987. Moreover, some jurisdictions have recently instituted or modified caps or other restrictions upon punitive damage awards (see, e.g., Illinois H.B. 20, effective March 9, 1995, which capped punitive damages at the greater of three times the actual damage or $50,000 and Texas S.B. 25, effective September 1, 1995, limiting punitive damages to $200,000 or two times economic damages plus an amount equal to any non-economic damages up to $750,000).

Data in this table are taken from "Punitive Damages Statutory Complication", Margaret D. Lineberry, Esq., Law Offices of Shook, Hardy & Bacon, Kansas City, Mo. (1992) and "Table 4-1 Summary of States' Positions on Punitive Damages", § 5.01 "Legislative and Judicial Definitions", and § 4.06 "Jurisdictions Prohibiting Punitive Damages" in Punitive Damages Law & Practice, James D. Ghiardi & John J. Kircher, Clark Boardman Callaghan Publishing (1996). It should be made clear, however, that errors or misinterpretation of the case and statutory law in this table are solely the responsibility of the authors of this report.

[2] Ala. Code § 6-11-20 (a).

[3] Cal. Civ. Code § 3294(c).

[4] Huelsmann v. Berkowitz, 568 N.E.2d 1373, 1378 (Ill. App. 1991).

[5] Biermann v. Gus Shaffar Ford, Inc., 805 S.W.2d 314, 322 (Mo. App. 1991).

[6] International Minerals & Resources, Inc. v. Pappas, 761 F. Supp. 1068, 1079 (S.D.N.Y. 1991).

[7] Tex. Civ. Prac. Rem. Code Ann. § 41.003(a).

[8] Ala. Code § 6-11-20 (a).

[9] Cal. Civ. Code § 3294(a).

[10] Menaugh v. Resler Optometry, Inc., 799 S.W.2d 71, 75 (Mo. 1992).

[11] Simpson v. Pittsburgh Corning Corp., 901 F.2d 277, 282 (2d Cir. 1990), cert. dismissed, 111 S. Ct. 27 (1990).

[12] Glasscock v. Armstrong Cork Co., 946 F.2d 1085 (5th Cir. 1991).

[13] First Bank of Boaz v. Fielder, 590 So.2d 893 (Ala. 1991). However, there is case law in Alabama indicating that nominal or compensatory damages are required to support punitive damages; O.K. Binding Co. Inc. v. Milton, 579 So.2d 602 (Ala. 1991), Gulf Atlantic Life Ins. Co. v. Barnes, 405 So.2d 916 (Ala. 1981).

[14] Cal. Civ. Code § 3295(d).

[15] Kemner v. Monsanto Co., 576 N.E.2d 1146, 1153 (Ill. App. 1991) (overturning a punitive award of $16,250,000 where the jury warded $0 for non-economic and $1 for economic compensatory damages).

[16] RSMo § 510.263(2).

[17] 105 East Second Street Assocs. v. Bobrow, 573 N.Y.S.2d 503 (N.Y. App. Div. 1991).

[18] Tex. Civ. Prac. Rem. Code Ann. § 41.004(a).

[19] Ala. Code § 6-11-21.

[20] Washington v. Farlice, 2 Cal. Rptr. 2d 607, 1 Cal. App. 4th 766 (1991).

[21] _Ekl v. Knect_, 585 N.E.2d 156, 164 (Ill. App. 1991).

[22] However, punitive awards may be reduced by any amounts previously paid by the defendant as punitive damages in other cases arising out of the same conduct (except in actions for libel, slander, assault, battery, false imprisonment, criminal conversation, malicious prosecution, or fraud); RSMo § 510.263(4),(5).

[23] However, punitive damages of $200,0000 that were 40 times the actual damages of $2500 were held to be excessive; _Manolas v. 303 West 42nd St. Enters._, 569 N.Y.S.2d 701 (N.Y. App. Div. 1991).

[24] Tex. Civ. Prac. Rem. Code Ann. § 41.007.

[25] In addition to the more tradition use of the term, Alabama law labels all awards in wrongful death actions as "punitive damages". _Black Belt Wood Co., Inc. v Sessions_ 514 So 2d 1249 (Ala. 1986). However, punitive damage awards in other types of actions are not considered compensatory in nature. See discussion of Alabama verdicts elsewhere in this report.

[26] Besides the purpose of punishment and of serving as an example to others, punitive damages in Texas "...also exist for the reimbursement of losses too remote to be considered as elements of strict compensation and for compensation for the plaintiff's inconvenience and attorney's fees. Thus, the application of the doctrine is widespread, as are the various purposes which serve to provide plaintiffs with cogent arguments for the imposition of punitive damages in different circumstances." _Punitive Damages Law & Practice_, Chapter 4, Page 5, §4.05 (footnotes omitted).

3. PUNITIVE AWARDS IN FINANCIAL INJURY VERDICTS IN CALIFORNIA; COOK COUNTY, ILLINOIS; HARRIS COUNTY, TEXAS; THE ST. LOUIS METROPOLITAN AREA, MISSOURI; AND NEW YORK: 1985 TO 1994

In this section we present our descriptive analysis of punitive damage awards in financial injury verdicts from jurisdictions in five states from 1985 to 1994. This section is divided as follows. First, we identify the statistical measures that we used in this analysis. Second, we analyze the entire database, including personal injury verdicts as well as financial injury verdicts. Third, we describe variation in punitive awards between different kinds of financial injury cases, between different jurisdictions, and over time. Next, we disaggregate the verdicts into these different kinds of financial injury verdicts and perform a more detailed examination on these groups of verdicts. Last, we estimate the effect of various punitive damage limits on the verdicts in our database.

STATISTICAL MEASURES OF PUNITIVE DAMAGE AWARDS

To identify trends in punitive awards in financial injury verdicts, we use several descriptive measures.

- *The number of punitive damage awards and the percentage of verdicts in which punitive damages are awarded.* Differences in the number of punitive awards and changes in the percentage of all verdicts in which punitive damages are awarded between case types, across jurisdictions, and over time may indicate differences in litigant and attorney behavior; they may also reflect changes in jury reaction to the cases brought to them over time.

- *The punitive award amount.*[1] Various statistical measures of the award amount, including measures of central tendency and variation, provide information about the size of the punitive

_____

[1] To control for inflation, we corrected all award amounts to 1992 dollars using the standard consumer price index.

damage award. We concentrate on the mean[2] and median[3] punitive award amount to provide information on the central tendency in the distribution of award amounts. We use the 90th percentile[4] punitive damage award amount to provide information regarding extremely high award amounts.

- *The relationship between amount of compensatory damages and amount of punitive damages.* Critics allege that punitive damages are high when compared to compensatory damages (economic[5] and non-economic[6] losses suffered by the plaintiff), and use this to argue that awards are unreasonable. For each case in which punitive damages are awarded, we calculated the ratio of punitive damages to compensatory damages.[7] We focus on the median of the distribution of this ratio.

ANALYSIS OF OVERALL DATABASE

First, to put punitive damages in financial injury verdicts in perspective, we describe the overall database used in this analysis. This analysis combines all verdicts from 1985 to 1994 from California;

---

[2]The mean award amount is the arithmetic average.

[3]The median award amount is the typical award amount because half of the award amounts lie above it and half lie below it.

[4]The 90th percentile requires additional explanation. Assume all cases in which punitive damages are awarded are ordered according to the amount of punitive damages awarded. The 90th percentile award amount is the award amount above which 10 percent of the award amounts lie and below which 90 percent of the award amounts lie.

[5]Economic damages include, for example, past and future lost wages, past and future medical costs, past and future property damages, or past and future lost profits.

[6]Non-economic damages includes, for example, pain and suffering, loss of consortium, and emotional distress. The amount of non-economic damages is also an important issue in the civil justice reform debate. Critics argue that non-economic awards are increasingly inappropriate when compared to the plaintiff's economic damages and injuries. This report does not address this debate.

[7]For example, in Case A the jury decides in favor of the plaintiff and awards that plaintiff $200,000 in compensatory damages and $400,000 in punitive damages. The ratio of punitive damages to compensatory damages for Case A is $400,000/$200,000, or 2.0.

New York; Cook County, Illinois; Harris County, Texas; and the St. Louis metropolitan area, Missouri.

This analysis indicates that the effect of financial injury verdicts in punitive damages for the jurisdictions in this study is similar to that observed for the fifteen jurisdictions used in previous ICJ research. Of the approximately 1300 punitive damage verdicts in the database used for this report, 50 percent occurred in financial injury verdicts. Within the population of financial injury verdicts, 14 percent of all verdicts were awarded punitive damages (See Table 3.1).

Table 3.1

Analysis of All Verdicts from California, New York, Cook County, Illinois, Harris County, Texas, and the St. Louis Metropolitan Area, Missouri, from 1985 to 1994

Case Type	No. of Verdicts	Plaintiff Verdicts		Punitive Damage Verdicts		
		No.	% of All Verdicts	No.	% of All Verdicts	% of Plaintiff Verdicts
Financial Injury	4,556	2,870	63.0	647	14.2	22.5
Intentional Tort	2,800	1,469	52.5	467	16.7	31.8
Auto PI	12,793	7,239	56.6	112	0.9	1.5
Landowner Liability	8,375	4,020	48.0	92	1.1	2.3
Medical Malpractice	5,238	1,681	32.1	28	0.5	1.7
Product Liability	2,224	876	39.4	46	2.1	5.3
Others	4,506	2,381	52.8	179	4.0	7.5
Overall[8]	35,556	18,024	50.7	1,304	3.7	7.2

VARIATION IN PUNITIVE AWARDS ACROSS MAJOR TYPES OF DISPUTES

Turning to the population of financial injury verdicts, we first categorized the financial injury cases in our database into major types of disputes, as described in Table 3.2. These types of disputes were chosen to highlight particular case types that are frequently raised in the debate over punitive damages. The first five categories all include disputes arising out of written, oral, express, or implied contractual relationships between the parties. We identified four particular contractual relationships because of their prominence in the debate over

---

[8]Number of verdicts, number of plaintiff verdicts, and number of punitive verdicts for the individual case types will not total to the overall numbers because each case in the data base was coded for each applicable case type. Therefore, one case could have been coded for more than one case type.

Table 3.2

Types of Disputes in our Sample

Types of Dispute	Definition
Insurance	Disputes involving the existence, interpretation, or performance of an insurance contract.
Employment	Disputes arising out of an employee-employer relationship.
Securities	Disputes arising out of the existence of a security instrument, including stocks, bonds, and other instruments of finance or ownership. Includes stockholder derivative suits.
Real Property	Disputes arising out of the sale, lease, or improvement of real property.[9]
Other Contract	Disputes arising out of the existence of an express, implied, oral, or written contract between the parties not identified above.
Other Commercial	Financial injury cases arising out of noncontractual relationships between the parties. Largely anti-trust and unfair business practice cases.

punitive damages. The fifth category captures all other contractual relationships that were not identified. Examples of contractual relationships that would fall into this category are endless, but include bank transactions, consumer transactions, and most business transactions.

The sixth category includes disputes arising out of noncontractual relationships between the parties. In particular, this category includes anti-trust and unfair business practice allegations between competitors, and brought by governments and consumer groups.

As Table 3.3 shows, within contractual disputes, most of the punitive damage awards were made in disputes arising out of three particular contractual relationships, insurance, employment, and real property.[10]

---

[9]*Real property* is land, and generally whatever is erected or growing upon or affixed to land.

[10]Even though 258 punitive damage awards are identified as *other contract*, this category is an aggregate of many types of contractual relationships with no single dispute type predominating. Overall, the

Table 3.3

Variation in Punitive Awards in Financial Injury Case Types (1985 to 1994)

Type of Dispute	No. of Verdicts	No. of Plaintiff Verdicts	No. of Punitive Awards	Punitive Damage Awards as a % of[11]		Punitive Damage Awards ($1992)			Median Punitive Award to Comp Award Ratio
				No. of Verdicts	Total Award Amount	Mean	Median	90th Per-centile	
Insurance	1,045	565	134	12.8	70.6	7,933,676	652,000	13,572,000	3.9
Employment	749	490	125	16.7	60.0	2,689,033	194,180	2,060,200	1.2
Securities	29	10	6	20.9	90.4	30,269,389	1,229,080	174,342,000	1.5
Real Property	978	650	113	11.6	46.0	2,110,888	94,700	2,048,000	0.9
Other Contracts	1,725	1129	258	15.0	43.0	6,283,804	277,875	8,423,360	1.2
Other Commercial	30	26	11	36.1	54.3	1,654,966	956,470	3,370,840	2.9
Overall	4556	2870	647	14.2	52.5	5,344,876	250,000	6,223,400	1.4

However, this does not mean that that these are the case types in which a punitive damage award is most likely. For example, even though there are relatively few punitive awards in the "other commercial" case type (11), this represents over 36 percent of all verdicts within this type of dispute.[12] Plaintiffs win less frequently in insurance cases than in employment, real property, or other contract cases. However, when they win, plaintiffs receive punitive awards less often in real property cases than in insurance, employment, and other contract cases.

Table 3.3 also shows that punitive award amounts are quite high and vary from case type to case type--the mean award amount varies from $2.1 million in real property verdicts to $7.9 million in insurance disputes.[13] The 90th percentile punitive damage award amount ranges

---

number of verdicts for any given type of contractual relationship in this category is quite small.

[11]These percentages, in this chart and in all other charts, are estimates of the true percentages because we are sampling from our entire database to provide these statistical measures. See Appendix A.

[12]Within insurance, employment, real property, and other contract case types, punitive damages were awarded in between 17 and 26 percent of plaintiff verdicts.

[13]The mean award for securities dispute is considerably higher than that in the other case type categories. However, because there were

from $2.0 million in real property verdicts to $13.6 million in insurance verdicts. In some distributions of punitive award amounts the mean award amount is higher than the 90th percentile award amount. This relationship between the mean of the distribution and the 90th percentile of the distribution indicates that there are a few punitive damage award amounts that are much higher than the rest of the awards in the distribution. Uniformly, punitive damages represent a large portion of the total amount of damages awarded (this includes verdicts in which punitive damages are awarded and verdicts in which punitive damages are not awarded): from 43 percent of all damages in other contract verdicts to over 70 percent of all damages in insurance verdicts.[14]

The relationship between the amount of compensatory damages awarded and the amount of punitive damages awarded in any given case has been a focus of the policy debate. Federal and state judiciaries[15] and legislatures[16] use the amount of compensatory damages awarded in a verdict as one factor in judging whether the amount of punitive damages awarded in that case is reasonable. We use the ratio of punitive damages to compensatory damages for each case to explore the relative size of punitive damage award amount for these case types.

Table 3.3 shows the variation in the median of this ratio across these case types. The highest median ratio is found in insurance verdicts; the lowest in real property verdicts. In insurance verdicts, at the median, the amount of punitive damages awarded is almost 4 times as large as the compensatory damages awarded. In real property cases, the amount of punitive damages awarded is slightly less than the amount

---

very few securities verdicts in our sample, the mean is sensitive to very high award amounts, and this likely reflects this. For this reason we are not holding this statistic to be necessarily representative of securities cases not included in our database. Similarly, other commercial verdicts displays the lowest mean punitive damage award amount among the case types. However, there were very few such cases in our database, and we are not confident that our analysis of this category of cases reflects cases not in our database.

[14]Again, because of the extremely low number of securities awards we do not include them in this discussion.

[15]See, e.g., BMW of North America, Inc., v. Gore, 115 S. Ct. 1589 (1996).

[16]Many states have imposed limits on punitive damages allowed in a case related to the amount of compensatory damages awarded in the cases.

of punitive damages awarded. This suggests that juries in insurance cases tend to reach higher punitive damage awards relative to the compensatory damages awarded than those hearing other types of cases.

VARIATION IN PUNITIVE AWARDS BETWEEN JURISDICTIONS

We next examine variation in punitive damage awards in financial injury cases between the different jurisdictions in our database. Table 3.4 provides the details of this analysis.

At first glance, this analysis suggests that punitive damages in financial injury cases is a California phenomenon--over 66 percent of these punitive damages awards were made in California. This is partly a result of the fact that there are more California verdicts overall in the database. When one compares the percentage of cases in which punitive damages are awarded between the states, California juries still have a higher propensity to award punitive damages. A plaintiff recovers a punitive damage award in 14 percent of all financial injury verdicts in Harris County. In Cook County, New York, and the metropolitan St. Louis area, punitive damages are awarded in less than 10 percent of all verdicts. Plaintiffs win in over 60 percent of financial injury verdicts in California, Cook County, and the St. Louis metropolitan area. Plaintiffs win in less than 50 percent of the

Table 3.4

Variation in Punitive Damage Awards in Financial Injury Cases between Jurisdictions in 1985 to 1994

Jurisdiction	No. of Verdicts	No.of Plaintiff Verdicts	No.of Punitive Awards	Punitive Damage Awards as a % of		Punitive Damage Awards ($1992)			Median Punitive Award to Comp Award Ratio
				No.of Verdicts	Total Award Amount	Mean	Median	90th Per-centile	
California	2,051	1,378	429	20.9	50.6	5,844,685	355,800	7,210,700	1.5
Cook County	402	261	17	4.2	50.7	3,233,558	250,000	3,000,000	2.5
Harris County	930	428	130	14.0	63.5	6,669,497	206,314	8,335,000	1.0
St. Louis metro	768	568	55	7.2	17.4	357,229	37,050	592,800	2.3
New York	405	235	16	4.0	20.5	567,579	55,127	3,755,500	0.5
Overall	4,556	2,870	647	14.2	52.5	5,344,876	250,000	6,223,400	1.4

financial injury cases in Harris County. They obtain a punitive damage
award in over 30 percent of all plaintiff verdicts in California and
Harris County, but 10 percent or less in the other jurisdictions in this
study.

Punitive damage award amounts also vary between jurisdictions. The
mean punitive damage award is considerably higher in California ($5.8
million), Cook County ($3.2 million), or Harris County ($6.7 million)
than in New York ($568,000) or the metropolitan St. Louis area
($357,000). The 90th percentile award amount is quite high in Harris
County ($8.3 million) and California ($7.2 million). Punitive damages
represent an important portion of total damages awarded in California,
Cook County, and Harris County. Interestingly, when the punitive damage
to compensatory damage ratio is compared between the jurisdictions, the
metropolitan St. Louis area and Cook County have a median ratio higher
then California or Harris County. This comparison shows that even
though on some measures punitive damage awards are considerably higher
in California or Harris County than in the metropolitan St. Louis area,
on other measures punitive damage award amounts are higher in the
metropolitan St. Louis area than in California or Harris County.

VARIATION IN PUNITIVE AWARDS OVER TIME

Punitive damages are commonly held to be increasing over time. Is
this true of punitive damage awards in financial injury cases? Table
3.5 describes punitive damage awards in the entire population of
financial injury verdicts separately for the five-year periods 1985-1989
and 1990-1994.[17]

---

[17]We chose to use five-year periods to minimize the effect of year-
to-year statistical variation in this analysis. An examination of the
data annually indicated no important event or year that would explain
variation between the first and second five-year period, but instead
supported the overall trends between the two periods.

Table 3.5

Variation in Punitive Damage Awards in Financial Injury Cases over Time

Period	No. of Verdicts	No. of Plaintiff Verdicts	No. of Punitive Awards	Punitive Damage Awards as a % of		Punitive Damage Awards ($1992)			Median Punitive Award to Comp Award Ratio
				No. of Verdicts	Total Award Amount	Mean	Median	90th Percentile	
1985-1989	2,197	1,397	348	15.8	43.8	3,390,509	195,600	3,912,000	1.5
1990-1994	2,359	1,473	299	12.7	58.6	7,619,931	364,088	12,052,170	1.2
Overall	4,556	2,870	647	14.2	52.5	5,344,876	250,000	6,223,400	1.4

This analysis indicates that the number of punitive damage awards has decreased between these two five-year periods, both in absolute numbers and as a percentage of the overall number of verdicts. Table 3.5 shows that punitive damages were awarded in about 16 percent of all financial injury verdicts in the 1985-1989 period and in about 13 percent of these verdicts in the 1990-1994 period. Plaintiffs have won cases at a slightly lower rate in the 1990-1994 period (62 percent) compared to the 1985-1989 period (64 percent). In addition, the percentage of plaintiff verdicts in which punitive damages are awarded has decreased slightly from 25 percent in the 1985-1989 period to 20 percent in the 1990-1994 period.

Punitive damage award amounts have increased from the first period in our dataset to the second. The mean punitive damage award amount increased from $3.4 million to $7.6 million, and the median award increased from $196,000 to $364,000. The 90th percentile punitive award amount increased at a greater rate than either mean or median award amounts from $3.9 million to $12.0 million. In addition, punitive damages represent a larger portion of all damages, rising from about 44 percent of all damages awarded in the 1985-1989 period to nearly 60 percent of all damages awarded in the 1990-1994 period.[18]

_____

[18]A further analysis of changes over time within case types or state provides little additional information. Similar patterns of decreasing numbers of cases and increasing award amounts were found in most of the case types and states.

Though the amount of punitive damage awards is increasing, the median ratio of punitive damages to compensatory damages has actually decreased from 1.5 in the 1985-1989 period to 1.2 in the 1990-1994 period. This indicates that even though punitive damages represent a larger portion of the total amount of damages awarded in the later time period, there are relatively fewer verdicts in which the punitive damages awarded are large relative to the amount of compensatory damages awarded.

VARIATION IN PUNITIVE DAMAGES WITHIN CASE TYPES

We now turn to a more detailed analysis of the four types of disputes in which most of the punitive awards appear--insurance, employment, real property, and other contract. We have analyzed variation within these case types along various dimensions including the state, the legal theory upon which the plaintiffs' recovery is based, and the nature of the parties. We omit the "securities" and "other commercial" categories from this analysis because of the low number of observations in these two categories.

Insurance

First, we examined the population of financial injury cases in which an insurance relationship is at the core of the dispute. This category includes all forms of insurance: auto, life, health, comprehensive general liability, and other insurance relationships. We analyzed variation in punitive damage awards in insurance disputes between jurisdictions, legal theories (using the legal theories described in Table 3.6), and types of plaintiffs.

Punitive damage awards in disputes arising out of insurance contracts vary considerably between the jurisdictions in our database (Table 3.7a). Within our database, California has by far the highest percentage of verdicts in which punitive damages are awarded. Punitive damages are awarded in almost 30 percent of all insurance verdicts in California. Our database indicated no insurance verdicts in which punitive damages were awarded in Cook County or New York.

Table 3.6

Types of Legal Theories in Insurance Disputes

Plaintiffs' Legal Theory	Definition
Denial of coverage	Includes cases in which the plaintiff alleges that the defendant is wrongly denying the existence of insurance or that the type of loss is covered by the insurance contract.
Denial of claim	Includes cases in which the defendant admits that the plaintiff's loss is covered, but the plaintiff alleges that the defendant is wrongfully denying all or part of the plaintiff's claim for losses.
Fraud	Includes cases in which the plaintiff alleges that the defendant has materially misrepresented the terms of the insurance contract.
Litigation defense issues	Includes the improper denial of the duty to defend, improper management of the defendant's defense, failure to settle, and other issues associated with the defense of the defendant in a separate action against plaintiff.
Other bad faith	Includes other cases in which the bad faith of the defendant is alleged, but which are not otherwise set out above. Also includes cases in which the exact behavior being punished cannot be identified in the report.
3rd party insurer	Includes cases in which the plaintiff is suing an insurer other than his own for acts committed by the 3rd party insurer.
Other	Includes cases in which the contract between insured and insurer gave rise to a dispute, but bad faith on the part of the defendant is not alleged.

In addition, punitive damage award amounts were quite high in California. The 90th percentile punitive damage award was $15.4 million, the mean punitive damage award was $9.1 million, and the median punitive damage award was $890,000. Punitive damages represented over 75 percent of all damages awarded in insurance disputes.

Punitive damage awards were high relative to the compensatory awards in insurance verdicts in California; the median ratio of punitive damages to compensatory damages was 4.8.

Table 3.7a

Variation in Punitive Damage Awards in Insurance Cases among Jurisdictions from 1985-94

| Jurisdiction | No. of Punitive Awards | Punitive Damage Awards as a % of | | Punitive Damage Awards ($1992) | | | Median Punitive Award to Comp Award Ratio |
		No. of Verdicts	Total Award Amount	Mean	Median	90th Per-centile	
California	116	29.7	75.6	9,107,182	889,500	15,451,500	4.8
Cook County	0	N/A	N/A	N/A	N/A	N/A	N/A
Harris County	14	6.3	14.3	491,691	46,963	1,024,000	1.1
St. Louis metro	4	1.8	0.1	12,055	11,882	18,525	1.8
New York	0	N/A	N/A	N/A	N/A	N/A	N/A
Overall	134	12.8	70.6	7,933,676	652,000	13,572,000	3.9

To evaluate variation in punitive damage awards in insurance disputes based on the legal theory used by the plaintiff, we categorized the verdicts using the legal theory upon which the punitive damage was awarded.[19] Table 3.7b provides the details of this analysis. This table shows that there was a considerable amount of variation in our

Table 3.7b

Variation in Punitive Damage Awards in Insurance Cases between Legal Theories from 1985-94

| Legal Theory | No. of Punitive Awards | Punitive Damage Awards as a % of | | Punitive Damage Awards ($1992) | | | Median Punitive Award to Comp Award Ratio |
		No. of Verdicts	Total Award Amount	Mean	Median	90th Per-centile	
Denial of Coverage	32	13.6	80.2	19,180,926	889,500	45,640,000	4.6
Denial of Claim	42	7.7	62.8	2,752,407	521,600	3,912,000	6.5
Fraud	15	21.6	84.9	5,611,517	71,720	12,361,200	1.1
Defense Issues	9	23.4	35.0	8,795,490	1,894,000	44,294,300	5.0
Other Bad Faith	17	29.2	66.3	2,645,185	652,000	8,738,100	3.8
3rd Party Insurer	16	67.9	84.4	6,695,256	1,257,500	18,525,000	3.1
Other	2	2.7	30.5	2,462,713	2,462,713	4,900,725	1.1
Overall	134	12.8	70.6	7,933,676	652,000	13,572,000	3.9

---

[19]The coding staff was instructed to identify the particular legal theory that was the basis for the punitive damage award in the case.

statistical measures among legal theories. It shows that the legal theories associated with the most punitive damage awards are denial of claim and denial of coverage disputes. However, among insurance cases, the highest percentage of verdicts in which punitive damages are awarded occurs in cases in which the plaintiff did not have a direct contractual relationship with the defendant insurer (labeled "3rd Party Insurer" cases in Table 3.7b).

Critics of punitive damages allege that they are being used inappropriately by some juries to transfer wealth from "deep-pocket" defendants to plaintiffs. To provide some information relevant to this allegation, we analyzed variation in punitive damage awards between individual plaintiffs and non-individual plaintiffs.[20] For this analysis, we have categorized the verdicts based on whether or not the punitive damages were awarded to an individual or non-individual. The non-individual category includes all non-individual parties: governments, businesses, and all other entities. We caution that we are not controlling for the facts of the cases in this analysis. It is possible that the facts of the cases in which the plaintiff is an individual are systematically different that the facts of the cases in which the plaintiff is a non-individual. Therefore, this analysis is inconclusive evidence about the "deep pockets" bias.

The details of this analysis appear in Table 3.7c. Individual and non-individual plaintiffs are receiving punitive awards in insurance disputes at approximately the same rate; 13 percent of the time for individual plaintiffs and about 12 percent of the time for non-individual plaintiffs. The mean punitive award amount is considerably higher for non-individual plaintiffs, $25.5 million to $4.5 million, as is the 90th percentile award, $45.6 million to $9.3 million. However, the median punitive damage to compensatory damage ratio is quite a bit higher for individual plaintiffs (4.4) than for non-individual plaintiffs (2.3).

---

[20]We acknowledge that this is an imprecise measure of wealth. Some business plaintiffs may be needy and some individual plaintiffs quite wealthy. However, it is the only tool available in our database to investigate this issue.

Table 3.7c

Variation in Punitive Damage Awards in Insurance Cases between Plaintiff Types from 1985 to 1994

Plaintiff Type	No. of Punitive Awards	Punitive Damage Awards as a % of		Punitive Damage Awards ($1992)			Median Punitive Award to Comp Award Ratio
		No. of Verdicts	Total Award Amount	Mean	Median	90th Per-centile	
Individual	112	13.0	64.7	4,479,438	652,000	9,340,995	4.4
Non-Individual	22	12.1	76.9	25,505,885	512,000	45,640,000	2.3
Overall	134	12.8	70.6	7,933,676	652,000	13,572,000	3.9

Employment

We performed a similar series of analyses for punitive damage awards arising from employment disputes. We analyzed variation in punitive awards between jurisdictions and between the legal theories upon which the plaintiff's award was based (using the legal theories described in Table 3.8).

The details of this analysis appear in Tables 3.9a and 3.9b. Interestingly, punitive damages are awarded in disputes arising out of employment contracts at relatively similar frequencies in four of the five jurisdictions represented in our database (see Table 3.9a). There were no punitive damage awards arising out of disputes regarding an employment contract from New York in our database. Punitive damages represented the bulk of all damages awarded in employment cases in California, Harris County, and the metropolitan St. Louis area. In the metropolitan St. Louis area, almost 90 percent of total damages awarded in employment cases was in the form of punitive damages.

Table 3.9a shows that the 90th percentile and mean punitive damage award amounts were considerably higher in California and Harris County than in the other jurisdictions in the database. However, the median ratio of punitive damages to compensatory damages was highest in Cook County and the metropolitan St. Louis area.

Table 3.8

Types of Legal Theories in Employment Disputes

Plaintiffs' Legal Theory	Definition
Race discrimination	Includes cases in which the plaintiff alleges that the defendant is wrongly denying an employment benefit because of racial discrimination, includes hiring, salary, promotions, termination, and other employment benefits.
Other discrimination	Includes cases not identified above in which the defendants behavior is motivated by discrimination against another protected class, including gender, age, or disability.
Violation of public policy	Includes cases in which the plaintiff alleges that the defendant has denied plaintiff employment benefits in a way that results in a violation of a public policy. For example, whistle-blower cases, or where the employee has rightfully sought benefits such as workers' compensation.
Fraud	Includes cases in which the plaintiff alleges that the defendant has materially misrepresented the terms of the employment contract.
Other bad faith	Includes other cases in which the bad faith of the defendant is alleged, but which are not otherwise set out above. Also includes cases in which the exact behavior being punished cannot be identified in the report.
Other	Includes cases in which the contract between employee and employer gave rise to a dispute, but bad faith on the part of the defendant is not alleged.

Table 3.9b describes the variation in punitive damage awards in employment disputes between the legal theories used to categorize the employment disputes in our database. This table shows that fraud actions exhibit the highest percentage of verdicts in which punitive damages are awarded (45.9 percent). However, the case type in which the highest portion of total damages awarded was in the form of punitive damages was race discrimination--almost 90 percent. In addition, cases alleging race discrimination violations exhibited a higher median ratio of punitive damages to compensatory damages than other case types (except for the other category).

Table 3.9a

Variation in Punitive Damage Awards in Employment Cases between Jurisdictions from 1985 to 1994

| Jurisdiction | No. of Punitive Awards | Punitive Damage Awards as a % of | | Punitive Damage Awards ($1992) | | | Median Punitive Award to Comp Award Ratio |
		No. of Verdicts	Total Award Amount	Mean	Median	90th Percentile	
California	88	18.7	60.6	3,306,723	214,600	2,608,000	1.1
Cook County	6	10.3	30.4	185,597	62,160	482,850	2.8
Harris County	18	17.2	52.7	1,766,707	236,750	5,858,840	1.1
St. Louis metro	13	16.9	87.5	926,915	91,280	896,000	3.6
New York	0	N/A	N/A	N/A	N/A	N/A	N/A
Overall	125	16.7	60.0	2,689,033	194,180	2,060,200	1.2

Table 3.9b

Variation in Punitive Damage Awards in Employment Cases between Legal Theories from 1985 to 1994

| Legal Theory | No. of Punitive Awards | Punitive Damage Awards as a % of | | Punitive Damage Awards ($1992) | | | Median Punitive Award to Comp Award Ratio |
		No. of Verdicts	Total Award Amount	Mean	Median	90th Percentile	
Race Discrimination	13	25.9	82.7	6,397,173	221,598	3,500,000	2.1
Other Discrimination	13	12.3	31.9	806,908	585,000	2,608,000	1.4
Violation of Public Policy	41	21.0	73.2	2,858,208	236,750	2,714,400	1.4
Fraud	16	45.9	57.0	6,995,233	346,518	5,858,840	0.6
Other Bad Faith	34	14.4	20.9	359,199	127,205	1,235,000	1.0
Other	9	6.8	10.4	162,812	91,280	544,525	2.3
Overall	125	16.7	60.0	2,689,033	194,180	2,060,200	1.2

Real Property

Next, we examine in more detail punitive damage awards arising out of disputes involving contracts associated with real property. We analyzed variation in punitive damage awards between the jurisdictions in our database and between the particular type of real property transaction underlying the dispute (using the transactions described in Table 3.10).

Table 3.10

Types of Transactions in Real Property Disputes

Type of Transaction	Definition
Landlord-Tenant	Includes cases in which the dispute arises out of a contract for the lease of real property.
Buyer-Seller	Includes cases in which the dispute arises out of a contract for the purchase of real property.
Agents	Includes cases in which the dispute arises out of an agency relationship regarding real property. This includes brokers and real estate agents.
Contractors	Includes cases in which the dispute arises out of a contract for construction on real property.
Other	Includes cases in which a contract involving real property gave rise to a dispute, but is not otherwise defined above.

Tables 3.11a and 3.11b describe in detail this analysis. Punitive damages are awarded in disputes arising out of real property contracts in each of the jurisdictions in our database. Punitive damages are awarded most often in California, with punitive damages awarded in about 19 percent of all real property verdicts. In addition, punitive damage award amounts were considerably higher in California relative to the other states in the database. The mean award was $2.9 million in California; the next highest mean punitive award is $226,000 in Texas. As noted above, the median ratio of punitive damages to compensatory damages is low within this case type relative to other case types. In addition, it is consistently low between states within this case type, ranging from 0.3 in Illinois to 1.5 in New York.

Table 3.11b describes the variation in punitive damage awards arising out of real property contracts between the types of transactions we have used to categorize these verdicts in our database. The percentage of verdicts in which punitive damages area awarded is highest in buyer-seller contracts for the sale of real property--almost 20 percent of all such verdicts--and lowest in contracts for construction on real property--4.6 percent of all verdicts. In addition, buyer-seller contracts are associated with the highest mean punitive award

Table 3.11a

Variation in Punitive Damage Awards in Real Property Cases between Jurisdictions from 1985 to 1994

| Jurisdiction | No. of Punitive Awards | Punitive Damage Awards as a % of | | Punitive Damage Awards ($1992) | | | Median Punitive Award to Comp Award Ratio |
		No. of Verdicts	Total Award Amount	Mean	Median	90th Per-centile	
California	82	19.1	50.0	2,855,187	107,300	2,472,384	1.0
Cook County	2	1.9	0.1	2,428	2,428	4,855	0.3
Harris County	12	8.3	24.6	226,498	48,207	150,000	0.5
St. Louis metro	9	4.8	4.5	74,111	16,000	468,696	1.0
New York	8	7.0	5.5	105,437	98,818	256,000	1.5
Overall	113	11.6	46.0	2,110,888	94,700	2,048,000	0.9

Table 3.11b

Variation in Punitive Damage Awards in Real Property Cases between Types of Transaction from 1985 to 1994

| Type of Transaction | No. of Punitive Awards | Punitive Damage Awards as a % of | | Punitive Damage Awards ($1992) | | | Median Punitive Award to Comp Award Ratio |
		No. of Verdicts	Total Award Amount	Mean	Median	90th Per-centile	
Landlord-Tenant	20	10.8	18.0	615,762	100,000	2,472,384	1.0
Buyer-Seller	47	19.9	70.4	3,825,219	84,825	1,080,511	0.9
Agents	27	13.4	33.9	869,738	53,120	1,073,000	0.7
Contractors	14	4.6	18.0	1,368,582	296,500	2,414,250	1.4
Other	6	12.0	28.2	1,050,695	97,800	5,200,000	0.7
Overall	113	11.6	46.0	2,110,888	94,700	2,048,000	0.9

amount, and the highest percentage of punitive damage awards relative to total damages awarded--over 70 percent.

Other Contractual Disputes

Last, we examined variation in punitive damages in other contract disputes. This category includes disputes arising out of numerous diverse contexts other than insurance, employment, or real property. We analyzed variation in punitive damage awards between jurisdictions, between legal theories upon which the plaintiff is seeking relief (using the theories described in Table 3.12), and between the individual or non-individual nature of the plaintiff and defendant.

Tables 3.13a through 3.13c describe the details of our analysis. Punitive damages are awarded most frequently in California and Harris County, but there are at least some punitive damage awards in each of the states in our analysis. Punitive damages are awarded in 6 percent of all verdicts in New York and Cook County and 18 percent in California and Harris County (see Table 3.13a). Mean punitive damage award amounts range from $161,000 in the metropolitan St. Louis area to $9.8 million in Harris County. The 90th percentile award amount varies from $350,000 in the metropolitan St. Louis area to $47.4 million in Cook County.

Table 3.12

Types of Legal Theories in Other Contract Disputes

Plaintiffs' Legal Theory	Definition
Interference with contractual relations	Includes cases in which the plaintiff alleges that the defendant is interfering with the plaintiff's ability to fulfill or enjoy the terms of an existing contract or to contract with others.
Breach of trust	Includes cases in which the plaintiff alleges breach of a fiduciary duty owed to the plaintiff by the defendant.
Violation of Deceptive Trade Practices Act (DTPA)	Includes cases in which the plaintiff alleges that the defendant's behavior violates the standards of the deceptive practices act within that state. Generally involves consumer relations.
Fraud	Includes cases in which the plaintiff alleges that the defendant has materially misrepresented the terms of the contract.
Other bad faith	Includes other cases in which the bad faith of the defendant is alleged, but which are not otherwise set out above. Also includes cases in which the exact behavior being punished cannot be identified in the report.
Other	Includes cases in which the contract gave rise to a dispute, but bad faith on the part of the defendant is not alleged.

Table 3.13a

Variation in Punitive Damage Awards in Other Contract Cases between Jurisdictions from 1985 to 1994

| Jurisdiction | No. of Punitive Awards | Punitive Damage Awards as a % of | | Punitive Damage Awards ($1992) | | | Median Punitive Award to Comp Award Ratio |
		No. of Verdicts	Total Award Amount	Mean	Median	90th Per-centile	
California	132	18.4	30.9	5,610,223	473,500	8,423,360	1.2
Cook County	9	6.2	61.9	5,983,560	500,000	47,350,000	4.2
Harris County	83	18.3	66.4	9,812,952	242,725	17,046,000	1.2
St. Louis metro	26	9.3	10.5	160,795	22,314	350,000	2.3
New York	8	6.0	50.1	1,029,721	42,540	3,755,500	0.2
Overall	258	15.0	43.0	6,283,804	277,875	8,423,360	1.2

Table 3.13b describes variation in punitive damage awards in other contract disputes between the legal theories used to categorize these verdicts in our database. As this table shows, most of the punitive damage awards were reached in cases based on breach of trust or fraud. Mean award amounts are high in interference with contract and other bad faith verdicts. The median ratio of punitive damages to compensatory damages was approximately one for each case type except for other bad faith cases, in which the median ratio was 3.7.

Table 3.13b

Variation in Punitive Damage Awards in Other Contract Cases between Legal Theories from 1985 to 1994

| Legal Theory | No. of Punitive Awards | Punitive Damage Awards as a % of | | Punitive Damage Awards ($1992) | | | Median Punitive Award to Comp Award Ratio |
		No. of Verdicts	Total Award Amount	Mean	Median	90th Per-centile	
Interference with Contract	29	22.7	58.8	11,685,711	970,900	32,190,000	1.5
Breach of Trust	53	42.6	62.3	8,196,962	521,600	17,046,000	0.9
DTPA	28	14.2	29.1	1,148,697	74,209	3,393,000	1.2
Fraud	99	29.2	46.5	2,717,231	212,628	4,564,000	1.4
Other Bad Faith	21	10.5	24.8	17,776,783	247,000	20,387,000	3.7
Other	28	3.8	55.9	6,127,042	256,637	20,000,000	1.0
Overall	258	15.0	43.0	6,283,804	277,875	8,423,360	1.2

Table 3.13c details the relationship between party type and punitive damage awards in other contract cases. For this analysis, we have categorized the verdicts based on whether the punitive damages were awarded to an individual or non-individual, and from an individual or non-individual. The category "other" includes all non-individual parties, government, business, or other entities. This table shows that in general the percentage of cases in which punitive damages are awarded does not vary greatly between the party type of plaintiff or defendant. It does suggest that an individual plaintiff receives a punitive award slightly more frequently that a non-individual. The data also suggests that punitive award amounts are higher in cases in which the defendant is a non-individual relative to cases in which the defendant is an individual.

The median ratio of punitive damages to compensatory damages is higher in verdicts in which the defendant is a non-individual (2.0 if the plaintiff is an individual and 1.5 if the plaintiff is a non-individual) than in verdicts in which the defendant is an individual (0.7 if the plaintiff is an individual and 0.4 if the plaintiff is a non-individual).

Table 3.13c

Variation in Punitive Damage Awards in Other Contract Cases between Party Types from 1985 to 1994

| Party Type[21] | No. of Punitive Awards | Punitive Damage Awards as a % of | | Punitive Damage Awards ($1992) | | | Median Punitive Award to Comp Award Ratio |
		No. of Verdicts	Total Award Amount	Mean	Median	90th Per-centile	
Individual v. Individual	64	16.0	32.9	787,138	128,763	1,600,000	0.7
Individual v. Other	103	18.2	54.8	3,832,969	195,600	8,423,360	2.0
Other v. Individual	29	14.2	24.5	761,875	194,180	2,841,000	0.4
Other v. Other	62	11.2	41.1	18,593,510	1,037,750	34,269,300	1.5
Overall	258	15.0	43.0	6,283,804	277,875	8,423,360	1.2

---

[21]The plaintiff is listed first; the defendant is listed second.

Again, we do not control for the facts of these cases. We assume
that cases involving individuals are likely quite different from those
involving non-individuals. Therefore, this analysis provides
inconclusive evidence regarding a "deep pockets" bias.

ESTIMATED EFFECT OF CAPS ON PUNITIVE DAMAGE AWARDS

One civil justice reform measure debated at all levels of
government is a cap on punitive damage awards. Many states have already
approved caps[22] and similar measures are being considered in other
states and at the federal level. Moreover, other states, such as
Washington, have banned punitive damage awards by common law or by
statute. To provide some context for the policy debate, we estimated
the effect of a cap on the existing financial injury punitive awards in
our database.

While many states have proposed or enacted caps at various limits,
from absolute monetary limits to numerous multiples of the compensatory

---

[22] In her dissent in BMW of North America, Inc., v. Gore, 116 S. Ct.
1589, Justice Ginsburg listed those states which had approved caps on
punitive damages as of May 1996. Those states are:

Colorado--Colo. Rev. Stat. §§ 13-21-102(1)(a) and (3) (1987) (caps
punitive damages at amount of actual damages);

Connecticut--Conn. Gen. Stat. § 52-240b (1995) (caps punitive
damages at twice compensatory damages in products liability cases);

Florida--Fla. Stat. §§ 768.73(1)(a) and (b) (Supp. 1992) (caps
punitive damages at three times compensatory damages);

Georgia--Ga. Code Ann. @ 51-12-5.1 (Supp. 1995) (caps punitive
damages at $ 250,000 in some tort actions; prohibits multiple awards
stemming from the same predicate conduct in products liability actions);

Illinois--H. 20, 89th Gen. Ass. 1995-1996 Reg. Sess. (enacted Mar.
9, 1995) (caps punitive damages at three times economic damages);

Indiana--H. 1741, 109th Reg. Sess. (enacted Apr. 26, 1995) (caps
punitive damages at greater of three times compensatory damages, or $
50,000);

Kansas--Kan. Stat. Ann. @@ 60-3701(e) and (f) (1994) (in general,
caps punitive damages at lesser of defendant's annual gross income, or $
5 million);

Nevada--Nev. Rev. Stat. @ 42.005(1) (1993) (caps punitive damages
at three times compensatory damages if compensatory damages equal $
100,000 or more, and at $ 300,000 if the compensatory damages are less
than $ 100,000);

New Jersey--S. 1496, 206th Leg., 2d Ann. Sess. (1995) (caps
punitive damages at greater of five times compensatory damages, or $
350,000, in certain tort cases).

damages, there is no agreement on what level is appropriate. The Supreme Court has recently spoken on this issue, ruling that while no bright line rule marks the limits of excessiveness in punitive damages, "a comparison between the compensatory award and the punitive award is significant."[23]

We chose to analyze the effect of a measure that would have limited a punitive damage award in any given case at different multiples of the compensatory damages awarded in the case.[24] This effect would have been in addition to that caused by any existing legislation affecting awards in our database.[25] The multiples chosen include one, two, three, four and five times compensatory damages. This array of proposals is consistent with legislative efforts in many states. In addition, we include an analysis of the effects of a cap at ten times compensatory damages. Although this measure is not to our knowledge being considered by any legislature, it provides a comparison to a very high cap.

Table 3.14 provides the details of this analysis using data from California; New York; Cook County, Illinois; Harris County, Texas; and the metropolitan St. Louis area, Missouri, over the ten-year period. This analysis indicates that if punitive damages had been capped at the amount of compensatory damages in each case, out of 647 punitive damage

---

[23]BMW of North America, Inc., v. Gore, 116 S. Ct. 1589 (1996). In BMW, the Supreme Court described three factors which are relevant to determining the constitutionality of a punitive damage award; 1) the degree of reprehensibility associated with the defendant's conduct, 2) the ratio between the plaintiff's compensatory damages and the amount of the punitive damages, and 3) the difference between the punitive damage award and the civil or criminal sanctions that could be imposed for comparable misconduct. The Court went to great pains to emphasize that no clear line demarcates excessive punitive damage awards from appropriate, but instead that a balance of these factors must be met.

[24]We acknowledge that most limits on punitive damage award amounts are structured as limits at a multiple of compensatory damages or some absolute level, whichever is higher. For the sake of simplicity, we estimated the effect of a cap at various multiples of compensatory damages only.

[25]Texas imposed a cap of four times compensatory damages or $200,000, whichever is greater, except in cases involving malice or intentional tort in 1987. Most of the data in our database from Harris County are subject to this legislation. Consequently, for Harris County our estimate is the effect of imposing caps beyond the cap already in place.

Table 3.14

Estimated Effect of Caps on Punitive Damages in Financial Injury Verdicts

Level of Limit (multiples of compensatory damages)	No. of Punitive Awards Affected	% of Punitive Awards Affected	Decrease of Aggregate Total Award (%)	Decrease of Aggregate Punitive Award (%)
1	386	60	43	66
2	280	43	34	51
3	219	34	27	40
4	184	28	22	33
5	168	26	19	27
10	102	16	10	12

awards, 60 percent, or 386, would have been affected. If punitive awards in these cases had been capped at the amount of compensatory damages, the total amount of punitive damages awarded would have been reduced by 66 percent. The total damages awarded would have been reduced by over 40 percent.

By comparison, if a cap at higher levels had been imposed, fewer punitive awards and a smaller percentage of the damages awarded would have been affected. For example, Table 3.14 shows that if punitive damages are limited to ten times compensatory damages, punitive awards in 16 percent of financial injury cases would have been affected. This would have reduced the total amount of dollars awarded by 10 percent. The total amount of punitive damages awarded would have been reduced by 12 percent.

For a number of reasons, we are not suggesting with this analysis that the experience in the jurisdictions in our database would necessarily have been as we estimate if punitive damages had been capped. First, our analysis does not take into account how such legislation would affect claiming and settlement behavior. Because of this, the mix of cases reaching juries under a different regime would likely have been much different from the mix we are analyzing. Second, juries may take into account limits on punitive damages in their calculation of compensatory damages, again leading to different outcomes than those actually observed. Therefore, both party and jury behavior would likely be quite different than that currently observed in the presence of limits on punitive damage awards.

4. PUNITIVE DAMAGE AWARDS IN ALABAMA: 1992 TO 1997

INTRODUCTION

Rightly or wrongly, juries in the State of Alabama over the last few years have developed a reputation as being generous in awarding punitive damages. Highlighted by the multimillion-dollar verdict in BMW of North America v. Gore, 116 S. Ct. 1196 (1996), many of the largest punitive damage awards granted by Alabama juries have received national attention. Some believe that Alabama is out of step with the rest of the nation when it comes to assessing punitive damage awards against deep pocket defendants, especially when the defendant resides primarily out of state.[1] Moreover, there is a concern that the size of many Alabama punitive awards are out of proportion to the underlying compensatory damages assessment.

We have undertaken a preliminary analysis of punitive damage verdicts awarded by Alabama trial juries, focusing on financial injury cases. We are reporting on these data separately because there are a number of important distinctions between these data and the data on the other five states in this report.[2] Data from Alabama reflect verdicts from 1992 to 1997, different years than those from the other states in our database. In addition, the data have less detail than those from the other states, and we are incapable of disaggregating the cases into the same detail as the other data.

---

[1]Professor George Priest of Yale University has studied the frequency and magnitude of punitive damage awards assessed by Alabama juries against out-of-state corporate defendants relative to their domestic counterparts. He concluded that out-of-state defendants are treated "unequally, indeed, grossly unequally" in terms of how punitive damages are awarded. See, e.g., Affidavit of George L. Priest filed April 15, 1996, in Scott, et al. v. New York Life Insurance Company, et al., CV 95-2269, Circuit Court of Jefferson County, Alabama.

[2]Appendix B provides the details of the methodology used in gathering the data reporting outcomes in Alabama jury verdicts.

PUNITIVE DAMAGE AWARDS IN FINANCIAL INJURY CASES IN ALABAMA

The balance of this section focuses on Alabama jury verdicts in financial injury cases, in particular punitive damage awards in these cases.[3] To facilitate comparison we will use the same set of descriptive statistics as those used to analyze the other states in our dataset.

The data from the Alabama courts reflect a procedural rule that requires explanation. Determining the rate in which punitive damages were awarded in Alabama trials is complicated by the ability of a jury to grant a special type of damages labeled as "general" to successful plaintiffs. These awards do not distinguish any punitive and compensatory components. In cases for which our data identify the type of awards granted by the jury, punitive damages were awarded in 16.7 percent of all verdicts, only compensatory damages were granted in 39.8 percent of all verdicts, and non-specific "general" damages awarded in 14.8 percent of all verdicts. The remaining 28.7 percent of all verdicts are defense verdicts.

The frequency in which punitive damages are awarded in all cases is therefore dependent upon how these general damage awards are treated. On the one hand, the decision to seek a general verdict could imply that there did not exist sufficient reason at trial to specifically label a component of the award as punitive. If true, general verdicts can be viewed as being compensatory-only in nature and treated as such. If so, punitive damages were awarded in 16.7 percent of all verdicts. On the other hand, the decision to request a general damages award may be driven by a desire to seek an award commensurate with punitive damages but without the associated stigma or the procedural complications. This suggests that all general awards contain a punitive component, and should be treated accordingly. This assumption leads to a conclusion that punitive damages are awarded in 31.5 percent (16.7 percent plus 14.8 percent) of all financial injury jury trials.

Table 4.1 provides the details of an analysis of punitive damage awards in financial injury cases in Alabama. In this table, we provide

---

[3]Appendix B contains more information about the distribution of jury verdict awards in Alabama.

Table 4.1

Variation in Punitive Damage Awards in Financial Injury Verdicts in Alabama from 1985 to 1994

Assumption on Nature of General Damages	No. of Punitive Awards	Punitive Damage Awards as a % of		Punitive Damage Awards ($1992)			Median Punitive Award to Comp Award Ratio
		No. of Verdicts	Total Award Amount	Mean	Median	90th Percentile	
General Damages Treated as Compensatory Damages	52	16.7	80.1	945,000	91,000	1,893,000	5.2
General Damages Treated as Punitive Damages	98	31.5	86.3	540,000	37,000	947,000	5.2
General Damages Treated as Missing Data	52	21.1	85.4	945,000	91,000	1,893,387	5.2

an analysis treating general damage verdicts as entirely punitive in nature, entirely compensatory in nature, and as missing data. An analysis of the magnitude of general verdicts suggests that they are more similar to compensatory damage awards than punitive damage awards in amount.

As this table indicates, punitive damages were awarded in 16.7 percent of all financial injury verdicts under the assumption that general damage verdicts were entirely compensatory in nature and 31.5 percent of all financial injury verdicts under the assumption that general damages are entirely punitive in nature. The former rate is similar to California (20.9 percent of all verdicts) and Texas (14.0 percent of all verdicts).

As with the other states in our database, punitive damage award amounts can be quite high in Alabama. Depending on the assumption regarding general damage verdicts, the mean punitive damage award amount is between $540,000 and $945,000 and the median is between $37,000 and $91,000. Even the upper end of the range for the 90th percentile punitive award amount in Alabama is lower than that observed in four of the five other jurisdictions in our database (see Table 3.3). As indicated in Table 4.1, regardless of the interpretation of general damage verdicts, over 80 percent of total damages assessed against defendants in Alabama are punitive in nature.

This proportion of total dollars awarded as punitive damages is higher than that seen in other jurisdictions. The other jurisdictions analyzed in this report had a smaller percentage of the total compensation identified as punitive. As shown in Table 3.4, Harris County is closest to Alabama with just over 63.5 percent of total dollars awarded.

Much of the controversy surrounding the application of punitive damage awards lies in its relationship to the accompanying compensatory verdict. For each case in our dataset, we calculated the ratio of the punitive award to the compensatory award.[4] The median ratio of punitive damages to compensatory damages was higher in Alabama than in the other states in our database. The median ratio in Alabama was 5.2 compared to 1.4 for all other jurisdictions in our database.[5] The highest state measure among the other states in our dataset was 2.5 for Cook County.

ESTIMATED EFFECT OF CAPS ON PUNITIVE DAMAGES IN ALABAMA

As we did for the other jurisdictions in our database, we estimated the effect of caps on the punitive damage awards in the Alabama data. As with our analysis of the estimated effect of caps on punitive damages in financial injury verdicts in the other states in our database, this estimate is additional to legislation already existing in Alabama.[6] For this analysis, we are assuming that all general damage verdicts are

---

[4]In seven verdicts not included in the analysis of the median punitive damage to compensatory damage ratio, a punitive damage award was reached without a compensatory amount indicated. It is unclear whether the compensatory award amount is zero or missing, or whether the jury was instructed to decide only upon the amount of the punitive award (as in a bifurcated trial).

[5]This reflects a considerable number of very high ratio awards. While 20 percent of the punitive verdicts were less than the amount granted for the compensatory award, 40 percent were at least ten times greater.

[6]Alabama law imposes limits on punitive damages at $250,000 except in cases involving a pattern or practice of intentional wrongful conduct or conduct involving actual malice. See Table 2.1. For Alabama, our estimate is the effect of imposing caps beyond the cap already in place.

entirely compensatory in nature.[7] The caps we will use as analytic tools are one, two, three, four, five, and ten times compensatory damages.

As can be seen in Table 4.2, caps would have had a dramatic effect upon the dollar amounts awarded in financial injury cases in Alabama. For example, a three times compensatory cap would have limited the award amount in 60 percent of verdicts in which punitive damages were awarded. There would have been a 66 percent drop in the total amount of dollars awarded; there would have been an 82 percent drop in the total amount of dollars awarded in the form of punitive damage awards.

Again, for the reasons identified previously, we are not suggesting with this analysis, that had punitive damages been capped, the experience in the states in our database would necessarily have been as we estimate. It is also quite possible that such a cap would have an additional effect upon the underlying number of cases filed in the Alabama Circuit Courts since some matters might not be economically feasible to litigate from a plaintiff's standpoint if the possibility of a relatively large punitive damage award was reduced or eliminated.

Table 4.2

Estimated Effect of Caps on Punitive Damage Award Amounts in Alabama

Level of Limit (multiples of compensatory damages)	No. of Awards Affected	% of Punitive Awards Affected	Decrease of Aggregate Total Award (%)	Decrease of Aggregate Punitive Award (%)
1	36	80	73	90
2	29	64	69	86
3	27	60	66	82
4	24	53	63	79
5	23	51	61	77
10	18	40	54	68

---

[7]This is an appropriate assumption for two reasons. First, we have established that general verdicts are more similar to compensatory only awards than to awards in which punitive damages are awarded. Second, this assumption leads to a lower-bound estimate for the effect of a cap on punitive damages on the data in our database.

CONCLUSION

As noted above, direct comparison of data from Alabama jury verdicts with those from other states in our report is difficult. Nevertheless, it does appear that of the six states we have studied, Alabama juries sitting in judgment upon financial injury cases return the largest punitive damage awards in relationship to their compensatory verdict. While they do not appear to award punitive damages at a markedly greater frequency than we have seen in other jurisdictions, such awards very often are many times greater than the compensatory award. Whether this is due to unique characteristics of Alabama jury behavior and attitudes, a different mix of cases brought to trial than in other states, or differences in state law is unclear. Certainly further analysis is needed for a complete picture of the way in which awards are granted in this state. What is clear is that judgments arising out of jury trials for financial injury in the state of Alabama contain extraordinary punitive damage awards relative to compensatory damages.

5. FINDINGS AND CONCLUSIONS

The key findings of this descriptive study are summarized below.

FINDINGS REGARDING CALIFORNIA, COOK COUNTY, ILLINOIS, THE METROPOLITAN ST. LOUIS AREA, MISSOURI, HARRIS COUNTY, TEXAS, AND NEW YORK

- 50 percent of all punitive damage awards are made in cases in which the plaintiff is alleging a financial injury only and no injuries to either person or property.

- Within financial injury verdicts, punitive damages are awarded in 14 percent of all verdicts. The overall mean punitive damage award in financial injury verdicts is $5.3 million. The overall 90th percentile punitive damage award amount is $6.2 million.

- Almost uniformly, punitive damage represent a very large percentage of total damages awarded within financial injury verdicts. Overall, punitive damages represent 53 percent of all damages awarded in financial injury verdicts. Within subpopulations of financial injury verdicts, punitive damages can represent an overwhelming percentage of total damages awarded.

- Overall, punitive damage awards in any given case tend to be higher than the compensatory damages awarded. The overall median ratio of punitive damages to compensatory damages is 1.4. Within subpopulations of financial injury verdicts, the median ratio of punitive damages to compensatory damages varies from less than 1 to almost 4.

- Punitive damage awards in financial injury verdicts vary between case types. In the case types we identified, the percentage of verdicts in which punitive damages were awarded was highest in employment disputes (other than securities cases which has a very small number of cases), and lowest in real property disputes. The highest mean punitive award amount and highest median ratio of punitive damages to compensatory ratio occur in insurance disputes.

- Punitive damage awards in financial injury cases vary between jurisdictions. Punitive damage awards were awarded in the highest percentage of verdicts in California (21 percent) and Harris County (14 percent), and least frequently in New York (4 percent) and Cook County (4 percent). Harris County exhibited the highest mean punitive award amount ($6.7 million) and the metropolitan St. Louis area had the lowest ($357,000). In California, Cook County, and Harris County, more than 50 percent of all damages awarded were in the form of punitive damages. However, in New York and the metropolitan St. Louis area, 20 percent or less of all damages awarded were in the form of punitive damages.

- Punitive damage awards in financial injury cases vary over time. While the number of punitive awards reached has decreased as a percentage of all financial injury verdicts (from 16 percent in the 1985-1989 period to 13 percent in the 1990-1994 period), the portion of all damages awarded which is punitive in nature has increased. The mean punitive damage award amount has increased from the 1985-1989 period ($3.4 million) to the 1990-1994 period ($7.6 million).

- Whether the party is an individual or non-individual is not associated with how often punitive damages are awarded in financial injury cases. However, individual plaintiffs tend to obtain punitive damage awards relatively larger than non-individual plaintiffs, and individual defendants tend to pay relatively smaller awards than non-individual defendants. Again, because we do not control for the facts of the case, this should not be considered evidence of a "deep pocket" bias.

- Proposed limits on punitive damage awards would have a large effect on punitive damages award amounts in our database. Using a proposed cap on punitive damages of three times the compensatory award in that case, 34 percent of all punitive awards in financial injury verdicts would be reduced by some amount. The total amount of punitive damages awarded in financial injury cases would be reduced by 40 percent; the total award would be reduced by 27 percent.

FINDINGS REGARDING ALABAMA

- Alabama juries award punitive damages in financial injury cases at a rate similar to that found in other states in our analysis. Punitive awards are reached in between 17 percent and 32 percent of all verdicts; higher than the overall rate for all other states in our database (14 percent) but about the same as that found in California and Harris County.

- In terms of magnitude, Alabama juries generally award smaller punitive damage awards than in the other jurisdictions in our database: the Alabama mean and median (between $540,000 and $945,000 and between $37,000 and $91,000, respectively, depending on the assumption used regarded general damage verdicts) were less than the overall numbers ($5,344,000 and $250,000) and much less than the figures for California, Cook County, and Harris County.

- However, punitive damages constitute at least 80 percent of all dollars awarded in financial injury verdicts in Alabama. Thus, punitive damages have a much greater effect on the total amount of damages awarded by jury trials in Alabama than they do in the other jurisdictions in our database. Overall, such awards constitute about half of all dollars awarded in our other jurisdictions; only Harris County (64 percent) approaches levels found in Alabama.

- When they do decide in favor of such damages, Alabama juries more often award punitive damages that are large relative to the compensatory award. The median ratio of punitive to compensatory awards was 5.3, far higher than the overall rate of 1.4 for other jurisdictions and more than twice the rate of the next highest jurisdiction (Cook County at 2.5).

- This higher ratio of punitive to compensatory damages in Alabama means that most proposals for imposing caps on punitive awards as a multiplier of the compensatory award would have a much more dramatic effect than in the other jurisdictions in our database. For example, a cap of 10 times the compensatory would only reduce the aggregate total awards in our other jurisdictions by 10 percent; in Alabama, the aggregate would be more than halved.

Appendix

A. DATA COLLECTION METHODOLOGY FOR CALIFORNIA; COOK COUNTY, ILLINOIS; HARRIS COUNTY, TEXAS; THE METROPOLITAN ST. LOUIS AREA, MISSOURI; AND NEW YORK

DATA SOURCES

The data used in this report were collected from jury verdict reporters within the sample jurisdictions. These are private subscription newsletters for lawyers and litigants that report the outcomes of, and relevant information on, jury verdicts in their respective areas. This appendix describes each of the reporters, estimates their reliability as data sources, and details the methods used to record the jury verdict information in them.

DESCRIPTION

The jury verdict reporters used in this study and the jurisdictions on which they report are described below.

Jury Verdicts Weekly (JVW)—California

JVW describes verdicts reached in Superior Courts and United States District Courts throughout California. To obtain information, JVW staff identify cases reaching verdict from public records; they then mail questionnaires to each attorney of record. Coverage is most comprehensive in the large metropolitan areas. We use data describing jury verdicts from state courts of general jurisdictions from this analysis.

Cook County Jury Verdict Reporter (CCJVR)—Cook County, Illinois

CCJVR reports verdicts in the Law and Municipal Divisions of the Cook County Circuit Court and the United States Distinct Court for the Northern District of Illinois. Like JVW, CCJVR identifies cases reaching verdict through the public records available at the courts and mails questionnaires to each attorney of record. Again, we use data describing jury verdicts from state courts of general jurisdictions from this analysis.

Jury Verdict Reporting Service (JVRS)—the Metropolitan St. Louis area, Missouri

JVRS reports all jury verdicts reached in the St. Louis metropolitan area and portions of Missouri, in both state and federal courts. Reporter staff identify verdicts from court records obtained from each court; they then contact each attorney of record to collect the relevant information. Again, we use data describing jury verdicts from state courts of general jurisdictions from this analysis.

The New York Jury Verdict Reporter (NYJVR)—New York

NYJVR reports verdicts reached throughout New York state. Reporter staff use numerous sources to identify cases reaching verdict, including court records, legal periodicals, and local, state, and national nonlegal periodicals. They then obtain information from each attorney of record. Again, we use data describing jury verdicts from state courts of general jurisdictions from this analysis.

The Blue Sheet—Harris County, Texas

The Blue Sheet reports on all dispositions reached in the Houston metropolitan area in both state and federal courts. *Blue Sheet* staff identify disposed cases from court records; they then contact the attorneys of record for each action and collect the relevant information. Again, we use data describing jury verdicts from state courts of general jurisdictions from this analysis.

RELIABILITY

It is obviously important that the information obtained from the reporters be as complete and accurate as possible. We have used independent solicitation of information by the reporters as a test for reliability.

Because many jury verdict reporters rely on lawyers or parties to contact them with information, their descriptions of the disputes reaching verdict are probably incomplete and biased. The reporters used in this study independently identify all disputes reaching verdict from public records and contact with the attorneys of record for both sides for information. By actively reviewing the public records, these reporters attempt to ensure that their newsletters describe all the verdicts in their jurisdictions. The reporters themselves provided us with estimates of coverage ranging from 80 to 100 percent.

In addition, the information itself must be accurate. To ensure accuracy, these reporters (1) use information from both parties in each case, (2) reconcile any discrepancies, and (3) provide the parties with the opportunity to edit the descriptions before publication. Since each party has an incentive to prevent the misreporting of information by the opposing party, these procedures ensure that descriptions of the disputes and their resolution are accurate.

Researchers who used these data in earlier studies (Peterson and Priest, 1982; Shanley and Peterson, 1983) determined more precisely the reliability of the reporters for two locations. The authors of the studies sampled the public records in San Francisco County and Cook County to estimate the reliability of JVW and CCJVR. They determined that JVW described 84 percent of the jury verdicts in the sample and that CCJVR reported on over 90 percent. They also found that for San Francisco County, the reporter appeared to underreport small automobile accident and business cases relative to higher-value verdicts.

We believe that these reporters provide relatively reliable data. However, the data collection process should be kept in mind. In this analysis, the number of cases should be treated as a lower-bound estimate.

PROCEDURE

Each verdict reported in a newsletter is described in a short paragraph. Our database has been constructed over the past fifteen years using three different coding procedures. Different procedures were employed as the succeeding collection teams learned from those that came before. The main difference from one period to the next was a simplification of the data collected. However, efforts were made to ensure that the data collected were consistent between the periods.

The form used in the last collection effort is considerably less complex than those used in previous ICJ coding efforts. This simplified form was necessary to obtain comparable data across the large number of reporters used in that study. A simplified collection form ensures that identical data are collected in all the jurisdictions.

All collection processes were overseen by the RAND Survey Research Group, which trained a staff to read through the reporters and code the relevant information. The reporters were initially screened by the staff to identify the verdicts that were to be coded. Verdict descriptions containing information that could not be coded were identified, and these verdicts were coded by supervisors or by the author of this report. All completed coding forms were reviewed by a supervisor to ensure that all information was correctly coded.

SAMPLING METHODOLOGY AND WEIGHTS

Personal Injury Verdicts

Because there are so many automobile personal injury and landowner liability cases, these verdicts were sampled. The staff was instructed to identify all automobile personal injury and landowner liability cases during the initial screening stage. Then, every fifth automobile personal injury verdict and every fifth landowner liability verdict was coded. The analyses adjust for the sampling process by weighting the data. All automobile personal injury and landowner liability verdicts in which the award was over $500,000 were included in the sample.

Tort cases were not subject to the recoding process for the analysis in this report.

Financial Injury Cases

All financial injury verdicts in the reporters were coded by the survey research staff in previous data collection efforts. In the recoding process where additional data were extracted from the case descriptions, we included all financial injury verdicts in which punitive damages were awarded. For compensatory-only plaintiff verdicts and for defense verdicts in these case types, we recoded a sample of 26.5 percent of the cases and adjusted the weights for these cases accordingly.

California 1985 Verdicts

Previous ICJ coding efforts had already worked with about half of all California jury verdicts granted in calendar year 1985. These cases were not included in the previous data collection efforts that form the basis for the current report. Thus, California cases for that year are additionally weighted, on a county-by-county basis, to reflect the total number of verdicts known to have been published in the jury verdict reporter.

B.   DATA COLLECTION METHODOLOGY FOR ALABAMA

INTRODUCTION

Over the past few years, the Administrative Office of Courts (AOC) in the state of Alabama has maintained a central database of information on all cases filed at the Circuit Court level (the civil court of general jurisdiction) in each county. The AOC began this operation in 1992, and it has been phased in since then. They feel that the database wasn't fully capturing all counties until 1995, but cannot give precise estimates of the number of counties that were included in the electronic database from 1992 through 1994. These data are used largely for case management and court administration. However, they also provide a detailed source of information on the civil justice system in Alabama.

The data include information on the case and parties involved in the action. The database is collected by the clerk of the court on the basis of the pleadings filed with the court; the disposition of the case by the judge, jury, or clerk; and a civil case cover sheet filled out by the original filing party. Among other information, the database includes the case type, method of disposition, amounts awarded by jury or judge, and an indication of the party receiving the judgment of the court.

CREATION OF DATASET

Although the Alabama dataset contains a rich lode of information regarding each case filed in the state, it does not have the much more detailed description of the underlying dispute and characteristics of the parties found in the jury verdict reporters we employed for other jurisdictions. Given the difference, we attempted to interpret the information collected by the AOC so as to maximize comparability with the data collected for other states.

The case type designation scheme used by the clerk's office has undergone a number of revisions since the data were originally put into a machine-readable format. We developed a cross-walk applicable to each of the different versions of the Alabama classification protocols.[1] At the highest levels, we sorted the cases in the database into four groups: torts, financial injuries, miscellaneous matters (such as zoning issues, appeals from administrative agencies, forfeitures, and the like), and unknown.[2] To the extent possible, we also attempted to further divide the caseload into subgroups that reflect the more refined definitions used in our current analysis of the other jurisdictions.

For the present report, we limit our analysis to cases falling into the general categories of torts and financial injury. We exclude the miscellaneous grouping because it contains cases that ordinarily do not go before a jury for resolution. We also exclude the unknown group of case types since we can not say with any certainty what matters are being litigated or even if they are ones with the potential of being decided by a jury. We do not break out the Alabama data into case type categories finer than torts or financial injuries because we cannot clearly assign many of these cases to categories that mirror our work in this report and in other ICJ analyses of jury verdicts.

We selected only those cases in the database that were recorded as having been decided by a jury verdict and in which the successful party was known. It should be noted, however, that the counts of trials presented herein will undoubtedly differ from published numbers of yearly jury trial counts in the state of Alabama. To maximize comparability with our work in other states, we made a number of subjective decisions.[3]

_____

[1]As we have done with our other jurisdictions, cases presenting "hybrid" case types with elements of both financial injury and tort (for example, contractual disputes with allegations of bad faith or fraud) were considered to be financial injury cases.

[2]Looking only at cases where the final court action was indicated to be disposition by jury verdict, torts constituted 65.9 percent of all verdicts, financial injury cases were 21.1 percent of all cases, miscellaneous 7.4 percent, and unknown 5.6 percent.

[3]The Alabama data differ from the other states in our database in one important way. In a very few cases, the judge will alter or adjust the jury verdict. The Alabama database verdicts reflect these postverdict adjustments of the judge, which we have not included in the other states in our data base. However, like our other jurisdictions, the Alabama data do not contain post-appellate changes nor do they

1. We dropped all matters where the relief sought or granted was
equitable in nature (declaratory relief, injunctions, extraordinary
writs, etc.) and appeals from either a lower court or an administrative
agency since such actions are not heard by juries.

2. Juries in the state of Alabama can award monetary damages in
one of two ways: either as compensatory and/or punitive damages or as
an undistinguished general award. While the size of a general award may
be influenced by the same factors that go into the calculus for punitive
award creation (outrageous conduct of the defendant, a desire to set an
example, the need to deter like conduct in the future, etc.), our
database does not indicate whether a punitive award would have been
granted but for the decision to employ a general verdict scheme. We use
such awards as evidence of a plaintiff win and of total dollars awarded
but cannot use them conclusively in our analysis of punitive damage
incidence and size. Instead, we first assume that all general damage
awards are punitive in nature and analyze the data. We then assume that
the general awards are all compensatory in nature and analyze the data
again. From these analyses we create a range for punitive damage award
statistics in Alabama..

3. Actions for wrongful death in the state of Alabama also present
a unique challenge. An award for wrongful death is characterized by
state law as a "punitive" damage award, regardless of the nature of the
defendant's conduct. For purposes of comparison with jury verdicts from
other states, we attempted, to the extent possible in the AOC database,
to identify any action for wrongful death damages. In turn, in any
instance where a wrongful death action yielded an award for punitive
damages, we shifted such dollars to the compensatory award field.

4. On first analysis, the dataset provided conflicting information
regarding the victorious party in the action. In some cases, the
plaintiff was indicated as the winning party, but no relief was granted.
Discussions with court staff indicated that the field used to designate
the winning side was more reliable for determining the victorious party
than the fields for the amounts awarded. Our review of a sample of

---

reflect any private settlements between the parties after the verdict is
received.

cases where we had independent evidence of the amounts awarded supported this conclusion. Accordingly, our counts of "who won-who lost" come from the field reflecting the party receiving the judgment (present in every one of our selected verdicts) but our numbers of total dollars awarded are derived only from those records with known dollar amounts.

SAMPLING METHODOLOGY AND WEIGHTING

No sampling was performed on the data received from the Administrative Office of the Alabama Courts.

OVERALL ANALYSIS OF JURY VERDICTS IN ALABAMA

The end result of our selection process was a total of 2,027 jury verdicts (1,572 torts and 455 financial injuries). The AOC database has been in operation since the early 1990s but full and consistent implementation of the statewide judicial information system did not take place until later years, mostly, in 1995 and 1996 (see Table B.1).

Table B.1

Alabama Jury Trial Verdicts by Year and Case Type

Year/Case Type	Torts	Financial Injury	Total
1993	87	30	117
1994	298	107	405
1995	455	133	588
1996	563	150	713
1997	169	35	204
Total	1572	455	2027

Overall, plaintiffs won more often than defendants. In tort trials, plaintiffs won slightly less frequently, but in financial injury trials, plaintiffs won considerably more often than defendants (see Table B.2).

Table B.2

**Alabama Jury Trial Verdicts by Award Type
and Case Type**

Award Type/Case Type	Torts	Financial Injury	Total
Defense Verdict	797	133	930
Plaintiff Verdict	775	322	1097
Punitive Award	27	52	79
Total	1572	455	2027

REFERENCES

Calabresi, G., *The Costs of Accidents*, New Haven, Conn.: Yale University Press, 1970.

Chin, A., and M. Peterson, *Deep Pockets, Empty Pockets: Who Wins in Cook County Jury Trials*, Santa Monica, Calif.: RAND, R-3249-ICJ, 1985.

Daniels, S., and J. Martin, "Myth and Reality in Punitive Damages," *Minnesota Law Review*, Vol. 75, No. 1, 1990, pp. 1-64.

DeFrances, C., and S. Smith, *Contract Cases in Large Counties*, Washington, D.C.: U.S. Department of Justice, Office of Justice Programs, 1996.

DeFrances, C., S. Smith, P. Langan, B. Ostrom, D. Rottman, and J. Goerdt, *Civil Jury Cases and Verdicts in Large Counties*, Washington, D.C.: U.S. Department of Justice, Office of Justice Programs, 1995.

Garber, S., *Product Liability and the Economics of Pharmaceuticals of Medical Devices*, Santa Monica, Calif.: RAND, R-4285-ICJ, 1993.

Ghiardi, and Kircher, *Punitive Damages Law & Practice*, New York, New York: Callaghan Publishing, 1980.

Hensler, D., M. Vaiana, J. Kakalik, and M. Peterson, *Trends in Tort Litigation: The Story Behind the Statistics*, Santa Monica, Calif.: RAND, R-3583-ICJ, 1987.

Hensler, D., "Reading the Tort Litigation Tea Leaves: What's Going On in the Civil Justice System," *Justice System Journal*, Vol. 16, No. 2, 1993, pp. 139-154.

Hirsch, W., *Law and Economics: An Introductory Analysis*, New York: Academic Press, 1979.

Kakalik, J., and N. Pace, *Costs and Compensation Paid in Tort Litigation*, Santa Monica, Calif.: RAND, R-3391-ICJ, 1986.

Litan, R., ed., *Verdict: Assessing the Civil Jury System*, Washington, D.C.: The Brookings Institution, 1993.

March, J., and Z. Shapira, "Managerial Perspectives on Risk and Risk Taking," *Management Science*, Vol. 33, No. 11, November 1987, pp. 1404-1418.

Mnookin, R., and L. Kornhauser, "Bargaining in the Shadow of the Law: The Case of the Law," *Yale Law Journal*, Vol. 88, No. 5, April 1979, pp. 980-1057.

Moller, E., *Trends in Civil Jury Verdicts since 1985*, Santa Monica, Calif.: RAND, MR-694-ICJ, 1996.

Peterson, M., and G. Priest, *The Civil Jury: Trends in Trials and Verdicts*, Cook County, Illinois, 1960-1979, Santa Monica, Calif.: RAND, R-2881-ICJ, 1982.

Peterson, M., *Compensation of Injuries: Civil Jury Verdicts in Cook County*, Santa Monica, Calif.: RAND, R-3011-ICJ, 1984.

Peterson, M., *Civil Juries in the 1980s: Trends in Jury Trials and Verdicts in California and Cook County, Illinois*, Santa Monica, Calif.: RAND, R-3466-ICJ, 1987.

Peterson, M., S. Sarma, and M. Shanley, *Punitive Damages: Empirical Findings*, Santa Monica, Calif.: RAND, R-3311-ICJ, 1987.

Posner, R., *Economic Analysis of Law*, Boston, Mass.: Little, Brown, 1986.

Priest, G., and B. Klein, "The Selection of Disputes for Litigation," *Journal of Legal Studies*, Vol. 13, No. 1, 1984, pp. 1-55.

Redden, K., *Punitive Damages*, New York, New York: The Michie Company, 1980.

Shanley, M., and M. Peterson, *Comparative Justice: Civil Jury Verdicts in San Francisco and Cook Counties, 1959-1980*, Santa Monica, Calif.: RAND, R-3006-ICJ, 1983.

Shanley, M., and M. Peterson, *Posttrial Adjustments to Jury Awards*, Santa Monica, Calif.: RAND, R-3511-ICJ, 1987.

Shavell, S., *Economic Analysis of Accident Law*, Cambridge, Mass.: Harvard University Press, 1987.

ICJ PUBLICATIONS

OUTCOMES

General

Carroll, S. J., with N. M. Pace, *Assessing the Effects of Tort Reforms*, R-3554-ICJ, 1987. $7.50.

Galanter, M., B. Garth, D. Hensler, and F. K. Zemans, *How to Improve Civil Justice Policy*, RP-282. (Reprinted from *Judicature*, Vol. 77, No. 4, January/February 1994.) Free.

Hensler, D. R., *Summary of Research Results on the Tort Liability System,* P-7210-ICJ, 1986. (Testimony before the Committee on Commerce, Science, and Transportation, United States Senate, February 1986.) $4.00.

——, *Trends in California Tort Liability Litigation*, P-7287-ICJ, 1987. (Testimony before the Select Committee on Insurance, California State Assembly, October 1987.) $4.00.

_____ , *Researching Civil Justice: Problems and Pitfalls*, P-7604-ICJ, 1988. (Reprinted from *Law and Contemporary Problems*, Vol. 51, No. 3, Summer 1988.) $4.00.

_____ , *Reading the Tort Litigation Tea Leaves: What's Going on in the Civil Liability System?* RP-226. (Reprinted from *The Justice System Journal*, Vol. 16, No. 2, 1993.) Free.

_____ , *Why We Don't Know More About the Civil Justice System—and What We Could Do About It*, RP-363, 1995. (Reprinted from *USC Law*, Fall 1994.) Free.

Hensler, D. R., and E. Moller, *Trends in Punitive Damages: Preliminary Data from Cook County, Illinois, and San Francisco, California*, DRU-1014-ICJ, 1995. Free.

Hensler, D. R., M. E. Vaiana, J. S. Kakalik, and M. A. Peterson, *Trends in Tort Litigation: The Story Behind the Statistics*, R-3583-ICJ, 1987. $4.00.

Hill, P. T., and D. L. Madey, *Educational Policymaking Through the Civil Justice System*, R-2904-ICJ, 1982. $4.00.

Lipson, A. J., *California Enacts Prejudgment Interest: A Case Study of Legislative Action*, N-2096-ICJ, 1984. $4.00.

Moller, E., *Trends in Punitive Damages: Preliminary Data from California*, DRU-1059-ICJ, 1995. Free.

Shubert, G. H., *Some Observations on the Need for Tort Reform*, P-7189-ICJ, 1986. (Testimony before the National Conference of State Legislatures, January 1986.) $4.00.

_____ , *Changes in the Tort System: Helping Inform the Policy Debate*, P-7241-ICJ, 1986. $4.00.

JURY VERDICTS

Carroll, S. J., *Jury Awards and Prejudgment Interest in Tort Cases*, N-1994-ICJ, 1983. $4.00.

Chin, A., and M. A. Peterson, *Deep Pockets, Empty Pockets: Who Wins in Cook County Jury Trials*, R-3249-ICJ, 1985. $10.00.

Dertouzos, J. N., E. Holland, and P. A. Ebener, *The Legal and Economic Consequences of Wrongful Termination*, R-3602-ICJ, 1988. $7.50.

Hensler, D. R., *Summary of Research Results on the Tort Liability System,* P-7210-ICJ, 1986. (Testimony before the Committee on Commerce, Science, and Transportation, United States Senate, February 1986.) $4.00.

Hensler, D. R., and E. Moller, *Trends in Punitive Damages: Preliminary Data from Cook County, Illinois, and San Francisco, California*, DRU-1014-ICJ, 1995. Free.

MacCoun, R. J., *Getting Inside the Black Box: Toward a Better Understanding of Civil Jury Behavior*, N-2671-ICJ, 1987. $4.00.

_____ , *Experimental Research on Jury Decisionmaking*, R-3832-ICJ, 1989. (Reprinted from *Science*, Vol. 244, June 1989.) $4.00.

_____ , *Inside the Black Box: What Empirical Research Tells Us About Decisionmaking by Civil Juries*, RP-238, 1993. (Reprinted from Robert E. Litan, ed., *Verdict: Assessing the Civil Jury System*, The Brookings Institution, 1993.) Free.

_____ , *Is There a "Deep-Pocket" Bias in the Tort System?* IP-130, October 1993. Free.

_____ , *Blaming Others to a Fault?* RP-286. (Reprinted from *Chance*, Vol. 6, No. 4, Fall 1993.) Free.

_____ , *Improving Jury Comprehension in Criminal and Civil Trials*, CT-136, July 1995. $5.00.

Moller, E., *Trends in Punitive Damages: Preliminary Data from California*, DRU-1059-ICJ, 1995. Free.

_____ , *Trends in Civil Jury Verdicts Since 1985*, MR-694-ICJ, 1996. $15.00.

Moller, E., N. M. Pace, and S. J. Carroll, *Punitive Damages in Financial Injury Jury Verdicts*, MR-888-ICJ, 1997, $9.00.

_____ , *Punitive Damages in Financial Injury Jury Verdicts: Executive Summary*, MR-889-ICJ, 1997, $15.00.

Peterson, M. A., *Compensation of Injuries: Civil Jury Verdicts in Cook County*, R-3011-ICJ, 1984. $7.50.

_____ , *Punitive Damages: Preliminary Empirical Findings*, N-2342-ICJ, 1985. $4.00.

_____ , *Summary of Research Results: Trends and Patterns in Civil Jury Verdicts*, P-7222-ICJ, 1986. (Testimony before the Subcommittee on Oversight, Committee on Ways and Means, United States House of Representatives, March 1986.) $4.00.

_____ , *Civil Juries in the 1980s: Trends in Jury Trials and Verdicts in California and Cook County, Illinois*, R-3466-ICJ, 1987. $7.50.

Peterson, M. A., and G. L. Priest, *The Civil Jury: Trends in Trials and Verdicts, Cook County, Illinois, 1960-1979*, R-2881-ICJ, 1982. $7.50.

Peterson, M. A., S. Sarma, and M. G. Shanley, *Punitive Damages: Empirical Findings*, R-3311-ICJ, 1987. $7.50.

Selvin, M., and L. Picus, *The Debate over Jury Performance: Observations from a Recent Asbestos Case*, R-3479-ICJ, 1987. $10.00.

Shanley, M. G., and M. A. Peterson, *Comparative Justice: Civil Jury Verdicts in San Francisco and Cook Counties, 1959-1980*, R-3006-ICJ, 1983. $7.50.

_____ , *Posttrial Adjustments to Jury Awards*, R-3511-ICJ, 1987. $7.50.

Costs of Dispute Resolution

Dunworth, T., and J. S. Kakalik, *Preliminary Observations on Implementation of the Pilot Program of the Civil Justice Reform Act of 1990*, RP-361, 1995. (Reprinted from *Stanford Law Review*, Vol. 46, No. 6, July 1994.) Free.

Hensler, D. R., *Does ADR Really Save Money? The Jury's Still Out*, RP-327, 1994. (Reprinted from *The National Law Journal*, April 11, 1994.) Free.

Hensler, D. R., M. E. Vaiana, J. S. Kakalik, and M. A. Peterson, *Trends in Tort Litigation: The Story Behind the Statistics*, R-3583-ICJ, 1987. $4.00.

Kakalik, J. S., and A. E. Robyn, *Costs of the Civil Justice System: Court Expenditures for Processing Tort Cases*, R-2888-ICJ, 1982. $7.50.

Kakalik, J. S., and R. L. Ross, *Costs of the Civil Justice System: Court Expenditures for Various Types of Civil Cases*, R-2985-ICJ, 1983. $10.00.

Kakalik, J. S., P. A. Ebener, W. L. F. Felstiner, and M. G. Shanley, *Costs of Asbestos Litigation*, R-3042-ICJ, 1983. $4.00.

Kakalik, J. S., P. A. Ebener, W. L. F. Felstiner, G. W. Haggstrom, and M. G. Shanley, *Variation in Asbestos Litigation Compensation and Expenses*, R-3132-ICJ, 1984. $7.50.

Kakalik, J. S., and N. M. Pace, *Costs and Compensation Paid in Tort Litigation*, R-3391-ICJ, 1986. $15.00.

_____ , *Costs and Compensation Paid in Tort Litigation*, P-7243-ICJ, 1986. (Testimony before the Subcommittee on Trade, Productivity, and Economic Growth, Joint Economic Committee of the Congress, July 1986.) $4.00.

Kakalik, J. S., E. M. King, M. Traynor, P. A. Ebener, and L. Picus, *Costs and Compensation Paid in Aviation Accident Litigation,* R-3421-ICJ, 1988. $10.00.

Kakalik, J. S., M. Selvin, and N. M. Pace, *Averting Gridlock: Strategies for Reducing Civil Delay in the Los Angeles Superior Court*, R-3762-ICJ, 1990. $10.00.

Kakalik, J. S., T. Dunworth, L. A. Hill, D. McCaffrey, M. Oshiro, N. M. Pace, and M. E. Vaiana, *Just, Speedy, and Inexpensive? An Evaluation of Judicial Case Management Under the Civil Justice Reform Act,* MR-800-ICJ, 1996. $8.00.

Kakalik, J. S., T. Dunworth, L. A. Hill, D. McCaffrey, M. Oshiro, N. M. Pace, and M. E. Vaiana, *Implementation of the Civil Justice Reform Act in Pilot and Comparison Districts,* MR-801-ICJ, 1996. $20.00.

Kakalik, J. S., T. Dunworth, L. A. Hill, D. McCaffrey, M. Oshiro, N. M. Pace, and M. E. Vaiana, *An Evaluation of Judicial Case Management Under the Civil Justice Reform Act,* MR-802-ICJ, 1996. $20.00.

Kakalik, J. S., T. Dunworth, L.A. Hill, D. McCaffrey, M. Oshiro, N. M. Pace, and M.E. Vaiana, *An Evaluation of Mediation and Early Neutral Evaluation Under the Civil Justice Reform Act,* MR-803-ICJ, 1996. $20.00.

Lind, E. A., *Arbitrating High-Stakes Cases: An Evaluation of Court-Annexed Arbitration in a United States District Court*, R-3809-ICJ, 1990. $10.00.

MacCoun, R. J., E. A. Lind, D. R. Hensler, D. L. Bryant, and P. A. Ebener, *Alternative Adjudication: An Evaluation of the New Jersey Automobile Arbitration Program*, R-3676-ICJ, 1988. $10.00.

Peterson, M. A., *New Tools for Reducing Civil Litigation Expenses*, R-3013-ICJ, 1983. $4.00.

Priest, G. L., *Regulating the Content and Volume of Litigation: An Economic Analysis*, R-3084-ICJ, 1983. $4.00.

DISPUTE RESOLUTION

Court Delay

Adler, J. W., W. L. F. Felstiner, D. R. Hensler, and M. A. Peterson, *The Pace of Litigation: Conference Proceedings*, R-2922-ICJ, 1982. $10.00.

Dunworth, T., and J. S. Kakalik, *Preliminary Observations on Implementation of the Pilot Program of the Civil Justice Reform Act of 1990*, RP-361, 1995. (Reprinted from *Stanford Law Review*, Vol. 46, No. 6, July 1994.) Free.

Dunworth, T., and N. M. Pace, *Statistical Overview of Civil Litigation in the Federal Courts*, R-3885-ICJ, 1990. $7.50.

Ebener, P. A., *Court Efforts to Reduce Pretrial Delay: A National Inventory*, R-2732-ICJ, 1981. $10.00.

Kakalik, J. S., *Just, Speedy, and Inexpensive? Judicial Case Management Under the Civil Justice Reform Act*, RP-635, 1997. (Reprinted from *Judicature*, Vol. 80, No. 4, January-February 1997, pp. 184-189.) Free.

Kakalik, J. S., M. Selvin, and N. M. Pace, *Averting Gridlock: Strategies for Reducing Civil Delay in the Los Angeles Superior Court*, R-3762-ICJ, 1990. $10.00.

_____ , *Strategies for Reducing Civil Delay in the Los Angeles Superior Court: Technical Appendixes*, N-2988-ICJ, 1990. $10.00.

Kakalik, J. S., T. Dunworth, L. A. Hill, D. McCaffrey, M. Oshiro, N. M. Pace, and M. E. Vaiana, *Just, Speedy, and Inexpensive? An Evaluation of Judicial Case Management Under the Civil Justice Reform Act*, MR-800-ICJ, 1996. $8.00.

Kakalik, J. S., T. Dunworth, L. A. Hill, D. McCaffrey, M. Oshiro, N. M. Pace, and M. E. Vaiana, *Implementation of the Civil Justice Reform Act in Pilot and Comparison Districts*, MR-801-ICJ, 1996. $20.00.

Kakalik, J. S., T. Dunworth, L. A. Hill, D. McCaffrey, M. Oshiro, N. M. Pace, and M. E. Vaiana, *An Evaluation of Judicial Case Management Under the Civil Justice Reform Act*, MR-802-ICJ, 1996. $20.00.

Kakalik, J. S., T. Dunworth, L. A. Hill, D. McCaffrey, M. Oshiro, N. M. Pace, and M. E. Vaiana, *An Evaluation of Mediation and Early Neutral Evaluation Under the Civil Justice Reform Act*, MR-803-ICJ, 1996. $20.00.

Lind, E. A., *Arbitrating High-Stakes Cases: An Evaluation of Court-Annexed Arbitration in a United States District Court*, R-3809-ICJ, 1990. $10.00.

MacCoun, R. J., E. A. Lind, D. R. Hensler, D. L. Bryant, and P. A. Ebener, *Alternative Adjudication: An Evaluation of the New Jersey Automobile Arbitration Program*, R-3676-ICJ, 1988. $10.00.

Resnik, J., *Managerial Judges*, R-3002-ICJ, 1982. (Reprinted from the *Harvard Law Review*, Vol. 96:374, December 1982.) $7.50.

Selvin, M., and P. A. Ebener, *Managing the Unmanageable: A History of Civil Delay in the Los Angeles Superior Court*, R-3165-ICJ, 1984. $15.00.

Alternative Dispute Resolution

Adler, J. W., D. R. Hensler, and C. E. Nelson, with the assistance of G. J. Rest, *Simple Justice: How Litigants Fare in the Pittsburgh Court Arbitration Program*, R-3071-ICJ, 1983. $15.00.

Bryant, D. L., *Judicial Arbitration in California: An Update*, N-2909-ICJ, 1989. $4.00.

Ebener, P. A., and D. R. Betancourt, *Court-Annexed Arbitration: The National Picture*, N-2257-ICJ, 1985. $25.00.

Hensler, D. R., *Court-Annexed Arbitration in the State Trial Court System*, P-6963-ICJ, 1984. (Testimony before the Judiciary Committee Subcommittee on Courts, United States Senate, February 1984.) $4.00.

_____ , *Reforming the Civil Litigation Process: How Court Arbitration Can Help*, P-7027-ICJ, 1984. (Reprinted from the *New Jersey Bell Journal*, August 1984.) $4.00.

_____ , *What We Know and Don't Know About Court-Administered Arbitration*, N-2444-ICJ, 1986. $4.00.

_____ , *Court-Ordered Arbitration: An Alternative View*, RP-103, 1992. (Reprinted from *The University of Chicago Legal Forum*, Vol. 1990, 1990.) Free.

_____ , *Science in the Court: Is There a Role for Alternative Dispute Resolution?* RP-109, 1992. (Reprinted from *Law and Contemporary Problems*, Vol. 54, No. 3, Summer 1991.) Free.

_____ , *Does ADR Really Save Money? The Jury's Still Out*, RP-327, 1994. (Reprinted from *The National Law Journal*, April 11, 1994.) Free.

_____ , *A Glass Half Full, a Glass Half Empty: The Use of Alternative Dispute Resolution in Mass Personal Injury Litigation*, RP-446, 1995. (Reprinted from *Texas Law Review*, Vol. 73, No. 7, June 1995.) Free.

Hensler, D. R., A. J. Lipson, and E. S. Rolph, *Judicial Arbitration in California: The First Year*, R-2733-ICJ, 1981. $10.00.

_____ , *Judicial Arbitration in California: The First Year: Executive Summary*, R-2733/1-ICJ, 1981. $4.00.

Hensler, D. R., and J. W. Adler, with the assistance of G. J. Rest, *Court-Administered Arbitration: An Alternative for Consumer Dispute Resolution*, N-1965-ICJ, 1983. $4.00.

Kakalik, J. S., T. Dunworth, L. A. Hill, D. McCaffrey, M. Oshiro, N. M. Pace, and M. E. Vaiana, *An Evaluation of Mediation and Early Neutral Evaluation Under the Civil Justice Reform Act*, MR-803-ICJ, 1996. $20.00.

Lind, E. A., *Arbitrating High-Stakes Cases: An Evaluation of Court-Annexed Arbitration in a United States District Court*, R-3809-ICJ, 1990. $10.00.

Lind, E. A., R. J. MacCoun, P. A. Ebener, W. L. F. Felstiner, D. R. Hensler, J. Resnik, and T. R. Tyler, *The Perception of Justice: Tort Litigants' Views of Trial, Court-Annexed Arbitration, and Judicial Settlement Conferences*, R-3708-ICJ, 1989. $7.50.

MacCoun, R. J., *Unintended Consequences of Court Arbitration: A Cautionary Tale from New Jersey*, RP-134, 1992. (Reprinted from *The Justice System Journal*, Vol. 14, No. 2, 1991.) Free.

MacCoun, R. J., E. A. Lind, D. R. Hensler, D. L. Bryant, and P. A. Ebener, *Alternative Adjudication: An Evaluation of the New Jersey Automobile Arbitration Program*, R-3676-ICJ, 1988. $10.00.

MacCoun, R. J., E. A. Lind, and T. R. Tyler, *Alternative Dispute Resolution in Trial and Appellate Courts*, RP-117, 1992. (Reprinted from *Handbook of Psychology and Law*, 1992.) Free.

Moller, E., E. S. Rolph, and P. Ebener, *Private Dispute Resolution in the Banking Industry*, MR-259-ICJ, 1993. $13.00.

Resnik, J., *Many Doors? Closing Doors? Alternative Dispute Resolution and Adjudication*, RP-439, 1995. (Reprinted from *The Ohio State Journal on Dispute Resolution*, Vol. 10, No. 2, 1995.) Free.

Rolph, E. S., *Introducing Court-Annexed Arbitration: A Policymaker's Guide*, R-3167-ICJ, 1984. $10.00.

Rolph, E. S., and D. R. Hensler, *Court-Ordered Arbitration: The California Experience*, N-2186-ICJ, 1984. $4.00.

Rolph, E. S., and E. Moller, *Evaluating Agency Alternative Dispute Resolution Programs: A Users' Guide to Data Collection and Use*, MR-534-ACUS/ICJ, 1995. $13.00.

Rolph, E. S., E. Moller, and L. Petersen, *Escaping the Courthouse: Private Alternative Dispute Resolution in Los Angeles*, MR-472-JRHD/ICJ, 1994. $15.00.

Special Issues

Kritzer, H. M., W. L. F. Felstiner, A. Sarat, and D. M. Trubek, *The Impact of Fee Arrangement on Lawyer Effort*, P-7180-ICJ, 1986. $4.00.

Priest, G. L., *Regulating the Content and Volume of Litigation: An Economic Analysis*, R-3084-ICJ, 1983. $4.00.

Priest, G. L., and B. Klein, *The Selection of Disputes for Litigation*, R-3032-ICJ, 1984. $7.50.

Resnik, J., *Managerial Judges*, R-3002-ICJ, 1982. (Reprinted from the *Harvard Law Review*, Vol. 96:374, December 1982.) $7.50.

_____ , *Failing Faith: Adjudicatory Procedure in Decline*, P-7272-ICJ, 1987. (Reprinted from the *University of Chicago Law Review*, Vol. 53, No. 2, 1986.) $7.50.

_____ , *Due Process: A Public Dimension*, P-7418-ICJ, 1988. (Reprinted from the *University of Florida Law Review*, Vol. 39, No. 2, 1987.) $4.00.

_____ , *Judging Consent*, P-7419-ICJ, 1988. (Reprinted from the *University of Chicago Legal Forum*, Vol. 1987.) $7.50.

_____ , *From "Cases" to "Litigation,"* RP-110, 1992. (Reprinted from *Law and Contemporary Problems*, Vol. 54, No. 3, Summer 1991.) Free.

_____ , *Whose Judgment? Vacating Judgments, Preferences for Settlement, and the Role of Adjudication at the Close of the Twentieth*

Century, RP-364, 1995. (Reprinted from *UCLA Law Review*, Vol. 41, No. 6, August 1994.) Free.

AREAS OF LIABILITY

Auto Personal Injury Compensation

Abrahamse, A., and S. J. Carroll, *The Effects of a Choice Auto Insurance Plan on Insurance Costs*, MR-540-ICJ, 1995. $13.00.

——, *The Effects of a Choice Automobile Insurance Plan Under Consideration by the Joint Economic Committee of the United States Congress*, DRU-1609-ICJ, April 1997. Free.

——, *The Effects of Proposition 213 on the Costs of Auto Insurance in California*, IP-157, September 1996. Free.

Carroll, S. J., *Effects of an Auto-Choice Automobile Insurance Plan on Costs and Premiums*, CT-141-1, March 1997. (Written statement delivered on March 19, 1997, to the Joint Economic Committee of the United States Congress.) $5.00.

Carroll, S. J., and A. Abrahamse, *The Effects of a Proposed No-Fault Plan on the Costs of Auto Insurance in California: An Updated Analysis,* IP-146-1, January 1996. Free.

Carroll, S. J., and J. S. Kakalik, *No-Fault Approaches to Compensating Auto Accident Victims*, RP-229, 1993. (Reprinted from *The Journal of Risk and Insurance*, Vol. 60, No. 2, 1993.) Free.

Carroll, S. J., A. Abrahamse, and M. E. Vaiana, *The Costs of Excess Medical Claims for Automobile Personal Injuries*, DB-139-ICJ, 1995. $6.00.

Carroll, S. J., J. S. Kakalik, N. M. Pace, and J. L. Adams, *No-Fault Approaches to Compensating People Injured in Automobile Accidents*, R-4019-ICJ, 1991. $20.00.

Carroll, S. J., and J. S. Kakalik, with D. Adamson, *No-Fault Automobile Insurance: A Policy Perspective*, R-4019/1-ICJ, 1991. $4.00.

Hammitt, J. K., *Automobile Accident Compensation, Volume II, Payments by Auto Insurers*, R-3051-ICJ, 1985. $10.00.

Hammitt, J. K., and J. E. Rolph, *Limiting Liability for Automobile Accidents: Are No-Fault Tort Thresholds Effective?* N-2418-ICJ, 1985. $4.00.

Hammitt, J. K., R. L. Houchens, S. S. Polin, and J. E. Rolph, *Automobile Accident Compensation: Volume IV, State Rules*, R-3053-ICJ, 1985. $7.50.

Houchens, R. L., *Automobile Accident Compensation: Volume III, Payments from All Sources*, R-3052-ICJ, 1985. $7.50.

MacCoun, R. J., E. A. Lind, D. R. Hensler, D. L. Bryant, and P. A. Ebener, *Alternative Adjudication: An Evaluation of the New Jersey Automobile Arbitration Program*, R-3676-ICJ, 1988. $10.00.

O'Connell, J., S. J. Carroll, M. Horowitz, and A. Abrahamse, *Consumer Choice in the Auto Insurance Market*, RP-254, 1994. (Reprinted from the *Maryland Law Review*, Vol. 52, 1993.) Free.

O'Connell, J., S. J. Carroll, M. Horowitz, A. F. Abrahamse, and P. Jamieson, *The Comparative Costs of Allowing Consumer Choice for Auto Insurance in All Fifty States*, RP-518, 1996. Free.

O'Connell, J., S. J. Carroll, M. Horowitz, A. Abrahamse, and D. Kaiser, *The Costs of Consumer Choice for Auto Insurance in States Without No-Fault Insurance*, RP-442, 1995. (Reprinted from *Maryland Law Review*, Vol. 54, No. 2, 1995.) Free.

Rolph, J. E., with J. K. Hammitt, R. L. Houchens, and S. S. Polin, *Automobile Accident Compensation: Volume I, Who Pays How Much How Soon?* R-3050-ICJ, 1985. $4.00.

Asbestos

Hensler, D. R., *Resolving Mass Toxic Torts: Myths and Realities*, P-7631-ICJ, 1990. (Reprinted from the *University of Illinois Law Review*, Vol. 1989, No. 1, 1989.) $4.00.

_____ , *Asbestos Litigation in the United States: A Brief Overview*, P-7776-ICJ, 1992. (Testimony before the Courts and Judicial Administration Subcommittee, United States House Judiciary Committee, October 1991.) $4.00.

_____ , *Assessing Claims Resolution Facilities: What We Need to Know*, RP-107, 1992. (Reprinted from *Law and Contemporary Problems*, Vol. 53, No. 4, Autumn 1990.) Free.

_____ , *Fashioning a National Resolution of Asbestos Personal Injury Litigation: A Reply to Professor Brickman*, RP-114, 1992. (Reprinted from *Cardozo Law Review*, Vol. 13, No. 6, April 1992.) Free.

Hensler, D. R., W. L. F. Felstiner, M. Selvin, and P. A. Ebener, *Asbestos in the Courts: The Challenge of Mass Toxic Torts*, R-3324-ICJ, 1985. $10.00.

Kakalik, J. S., P. A. Ebener, W. L. F. Felstiner, and M. G. Shanley, *Costs of Asbestos Litigation*, R-3042-ICJ, 1983. $4.00.

Kakalik, J. S., P. A. Ebener, W. L. F. Felstiner, G. W. Haggstrom, and M. G. Shanley, *Variation in Asbestos Litigation Compensation and Expenses*, R-3132-ICJ, 1984. $7.50.

Peterson, M. A., *Giving Away Money: Comparative Comments on Claims Resolution Facilities*, RP-108, 1992. (Reprinted from *Law and Contemporary Problems*, Vol. 53, No. 4, Autumn 1990.) Free.

Peterson, M. A., and M. Selvin, *Resolution of Mass Torts: Toward a Framework for Evaluation of Aggregative Procedures*, N-2805-ICJ, 1988. $7.50.

_____ , *Mass Justice: The Limited and Unlimited Power of Courts*, RP-116, 1992. (Reprinted from *Law and Contemporary Problems*, No. 3, Summer 1991.) Free.

Selvin, M., and L. Picus, *The Debate over Jury Performance: Observations from a Recent Asbestos Case*, R-3479-ICJ, 1987. $10.00.

Aviation Accidents

Kakalik, J. S., E. M. King, M. Traynor, P. A. Ebener, and L. Picus, *Costs and Compensation Paid in Aviation Accident Litigation*, R-3421-ICJ, 1988. $10.00.

_____ , *Aviation Accident Litigation Survey: Data Collection Forms*, N-2773-ICJ, 1988. $7.50.

King, E. M., and J. P. Smith, *Computing Economic Loss in Cases of Wrongful Death,* R-3549-ICJ, 1988. $10.00.

_____ , *Economic Loss and Compensation in Aviation Accidents*, R-3551-ICJ, 1988. $10.00.

_____ , *Dispute Resolution Following Airplane Crashes*, R-3585-ICJ, 1988. $7.50.

Executive Summaries of the Aviation Accident Study, R-3684, 1988. $7.50.

Environment: California's Clean-Air Strategy

Dixon, L. S., and S. Garber, *California's Ozone-Reduction Strategy for Light-Duty Vehicles: Direct Costs, Direct Emission Effects and Market Responses*, MR-695-ICJ, 1996. $13.00.

——, *Economic Perspectives on Revising California's Zero-Emission Vehicle Mandate,* CT-137, March 1996. $5.00.

Dixon, L. S., S. Garber, and M. E. Vaiana, *California's Ozone-Reduction Strategy for Light-Duty Vehicles: An Economic Assessment*, MR-695/1-ICJ, 1996. $15.00.

——, *Making ZEV Policy Despite Uncertainty: An Annotated Briefing for the California Air Resources Board*, DRU-1266-1-ICJ, 1995. Free.

Environment: Superfund

Acton, J. P., *Understanding Superfund: A Progress Report*, R-3838-ICJ, 1989. $7.50.

Acton, J. P., and L. S. Dixon with D. Drezner, L. Hill, and S. McKenney, *Superfund and Transaction Costs: The Experiences of Insurers and Very Large Industrial Firms*, R-4132-ICJ, 1992. $7.50.

Dixon, L. S., *RAND Research on Superfund Transaction Costs: A Summary of Findings to Date*, CT-111, November 1993. $5.00.

_____ , *Fixing Superfund: The Effect of the Proposed Superfund Reform Act of 1994 on Transaction Costs*, MR-455-ICJ, 1994. $15.00.

_____ , *Superfund Liability Reform: Implications for Transaction Costs and Site Cleanup*, CT-125, 1995. $5.00.

Dixon, L. S., D. S. Drezner, and J. K. Hammitt, *Private-Sector Cleanup Expenditures and Transaction Costs at 18 Superfund Sites*, MR-204-EPA/RC, 1993. $13.00.

Reuter, P., *The Economic Consequences of Expanded Corporate Liability: An Exploratory Study*, N-2807-ICJ, 1988. $7.50.

Law and the Changing American Workplace

Darling-Hammond, L., and T. J. Kniesner, *The Law and Economics of Workers' Compensation*, R-2716-ICJ, 1980. $7.50.

Dertouzos, J. N., E. Holland, and P. A. Ebener, *The Legal and Economic Consequences of Wrongful Termination*, R-3602-ICJ, 1988. $7.50.

Dertouzos, J. N., and L. A. Karoly, *Labor-Market Responses to Employer Liability*, R-3989-ICJ, 1992. $7.50.

Victor, R. B., *Workers' Compensation and Workplace Safety: The Nature of Employer Financial Incentives*, R-2979-ICJ, 1982. $7.50.

Victor, R. B., L. R. Cohen, and C. E. Phelps, *Workers' Compensation and Workplace Safety: Some Lessons from Economic Theory*, R-2918-ICJ, 1982. $7.50.

Medical Malpractice

Danzon, P. M., *Contingent Fees for Personal Injury Litigation*, R-2458-HCFA, 1980. $4.00.

_____ , *The Disposition of Medical Malpractice Claims*, R-2622-HCFA, 1980. $7.50.

_____ , *Why Are Malpractice Premiums So High—Or So Low?* R-2623-HCFA, 1980. $4.00.

_____ , *The Frequency and Severity of Medical Malpractice Claims*, R-2870-ICJ/HCFA, 1982. $7.50.

_____ , *New Evidence on the Frequency and Severity of Medical Malpractice Claims*, R-3410-ICJ, 1986. $4.00.

_____ , *The Effects of Tort Reform on the Frequency and Severity of Medical Malpractice Claims: A Summary of Research Results*, P-7211, 1986. (Testimony before the Committee on the Judiciary, United States Senate, March 1986.) $4.00.

Danzon, P. M., and L. A. Lillard, *The Resolution of Medical Malpractice Claims: Modeling the Bargaining Process*, R-2792-ICJ, 1982. $7.50.

_____ , *Settlement Out of Court: The Disposition of Medical Malpractice Claims*, P-6800, 1982. $4.00.

_____ , *The Resolution of Medical Malpractice Claims: Research Results and Policy Implications*, R-2793-ICJ, 1982. $4.00.

Kravitz, R. L. , J. E. Rolph, K. A. McGuigan, *Malpractice Claims Data as a Quality Improvement Tool: I. Epidemiology of Error in Four Specialties*, N-3448/1-RWJ, 1991. $4.00.

Lewis, E., and J. E. Rolph, *The Bad Apples? Malpractice Claims Experience of Physicians with a Surplus Lines Insurer*, P-7812, 1993. $4.00.

Rolph, E. S., *Health Care Delivery and Tort: Systems on a Collision Course?* Conference Proceedings, Dallas, June 1991, N-3524-ICJ, 1992. $10.00.

Rolph, J. E., *Some Statistical Evidence on Merit Rating in Medical Malpractice Insurance*, N-1725-HHS, 1981. $4.00.

_____ , *Merit Rating for Physicians' Malpractice Premiums: Only a Modest Deterrent*, N-3426-MT/RWJ/RC, 1991. $4.00.

Rolph, J. E., R. L. Kravitz, and K. A. McGuigan, *Malpractice Claims Data as a Quality Improvement Tool: II. Is Targeting Effective?* N-3448/2-RWJ, 1991. $4.00.

Williams, A. P., *Malpractice, Outcomes, and Appropriateness of Care*, P-7445, May 1988. $4.00.

Product Liability

Dunworth, T., *Product Liability and the Business Sector: Litigation Trends in Federal Courts*, R-3668-ICJ, 1988. $7.50.

Eads, G., and P. Reuter, *Designing Safer Products: Corporate Responses to Product Liability Law and Regulation*, R-3022-ICJ, 1983. $15.00.

_____ , *Designing Safer Products: Corporate Responses to Product Liability Law and Regulation*, P-7089-ICJ, 1985. (Reprinted from the *Journal of Product Liability*, Vol. 7, 1985.) $4.00.

Garber, S., *Product Liability and the Economics of Pharmaceuticals and Medical Devices*, R-4285-ICJ, 1993. $15.00.

Hensler, D. R., *Summary of Research Results on Product Liability*, P-7271-ICJ, 1986. (Statement submitted to the Committee on the Judiciary, United States Senate, October 1986.) $4.00.

_____ , *What We Know and Don't Know About Product Liability*, P-7775-ICJ, 1993. (Statement submitted to the Commerce Committee, United States Senate, September 1991.) $4.00.

Moller, E., *Trends in Civil Jury Verdicts Since 1985*, MR-694-ICJ, 1996. $15.00.

Peterson, M. A., *Civil Juries in the 1980s: Trends in Jury Trials and Verdicts in California and Cook County, Illinois*, R-3466-ICJ, 1987. $7.50.

Reuter, P., *The Economic Consequences of Expanded Corporate Liability: An Exploratory Study*, N-2807-ICJ, 1988. $7.50.

MASS TORTS AND CLASS ACTIONS

Hensler, D. R., *Resolving Mass Toxic Torts: Myths and Realities*, P-7631-ICJ, 1990. (Reprinted from the *University of Illinois Law Review*, Vol. 1989, No. 1.) $4.00.

_____ , *Asbestos Litigation in the United States: A Brief Overview*, P-7776-ICJ, 1992. (Testimony before the Courts and Judicial Administration Subcommittee, United States House Judiciary Committee, October 1991.) $4.00.

_____ , *Assessing Claims Resolution Facilities: What We Need to Know*, RP-107, 1992. (Reprinted from *Law and Contemporary Problems*, Vol. 53, No. 4, Autumn 1990.) Free.

_____ , *Fashioning a National Resolution of Asbestos Personal Injury Litigation: A Reply to Professor Brickman*, RP-114, 1992. (Reprinted from *Cardozo Law Review*, Vol. 13, No. 6, April 1992.) Free.

_____ , *A Glass Half Full, a Glass Half Empty: The Use of Alternative Dispute Resolution in Mass Personal Injury Litigation*, RP-446, 1995. (Reprinted from *Texas Law Review*, Vol. 73, No. 7, June 1995.) Free.

Hensler, D. R., W. L. F. Felstiner, M. Selvin, and P. A. Ebener, *Asbestos in the Courts: The Challenge of Mass Toxic Torts*, R-3324-ICJ, 1985. $10.00.

Hensler, D. R., J. Gross, E. Moller, and N. Pace, *Preliminary Results of the RAND Study of Class Action Litigation*, DB-220-ICJ, 1997. $6.00.

Hensler, D. R., and M. A. Peterson, *Understanding Mass Personal Injury Litigation: A Socio-Legal Analysis*, RP-311, 1994. (Reprinted from *Brooklyn Law Review*, Vol. 59, No. 3, Fall 1993.) Free.

Kakalik, J. S., P. A. Ebener, W. L. F. Felstiner, G. W. Haggstrom, and M. G. Shanley, *Variation in Asbestos Litigation Compensation and Expenses*, R-3132-ICJ, 1984. $7.50.

Kakalik, J. S., P. A. Ebener, W. L. F. Felstiner, and M. G. Shanley, *Costs of Asbestos Litigation*, R-3042-ICJ, 1983. $4.00.

Peterson, M. A., *Giving Away Money: Comparative Comments on Claims Resolution Facilities*, RP-108, 1992. (Reprinted from *Law and Contemporary Problems*, Vol. 53, No. 4, Autumn 1990.) Free.

Peterson, M. A., and M. Selvin, *Resolution of Mass Torts: Toward a Framework for Evaluation of Aggregative Procedures*, N-2805-ICJ, 1988. $7.50.

_____ , *Mass Justice: The Limited and Unlimited Power of Courts*, RP-116, 1992. (Reprinted from *Law and Contemporary Problems*, Vol. 54, No. 3, Summer 1991.) Free.

Selvin, M., and L. Picus, *The Debate over Jury Performance: Observations from a Recent Asbestos Case*, R-3479-ICJ, 1987. $10.00.

TRENDS IN THE TORT LITIGATION SYSTEM

Galanter, M., B. Garth, D. Hensler, and F. K. Zemans, *How to Improve Civil Justice Policy*, RP-282. (Reprinted from *Judicature*, Vol. 77, No. 4, January/February 1994.) Free.

Hensler, D. R., *Summary of Research Results on the Tort Liability System*, P-7210-ICJ, 1986. (Testimony before the Committee on Commerce, Science, and Transportation, United States Senate, February 1986.) $4.00.

——, *Trends in California Tort Liability Litigation*, P-7287-ICJ, 1987. (Testimony before the Select Committee on Insurance, California State Assembly, October 1987.) $4.00.

_____ , *Reading the Tort Litigation Tea Leaves: What's Going on in the Civil Liability System?* RP-226. (Reprinted from *The Justice System Journal*, Vol. 16, No. 2, 1993.) Free.

_____ , *A Glass Half Full, a Glass Half Empty: The Use of Alternative Dispute Resolution in Mass Personal Injury Litigation*, RP-446, 1995. (Reprinted from *Texas Law Review*, Vol. 73, No. 7, June 1995.) Free.

Hensler, D. R., and E. Moller, *Trends in Punitive Damages: Preliminary Data from Cook County, Illinois, and San Francisco, California*, DRU-1014-ICJ, 1995. Free.

Hensler, D. R., M. E. Vaiana, J. S. Kakalik, and M. A. Peterson, *Trends in Tort Litigation: The Story Behind the Statistics*, R-3583-ICJ, 1987. $4.00.

Moller, E., *Trends in Punitive Damages: Preliminary Data from California*, DRU-1059-ICJ, 1995. Free.

_____ , *Trends in Civil Jury Verdicts Since 1985*, MR-694-ICJ, 1996. $15.00.

Moller, E., N. M. Pace, and S. J. Carroll, *Punitive Damages in Financial Injury Jury Verdicts*, MR-888-ICJ, 1997, $9.00.

_____ , *Punitive Damages in Financial Injury Jury Verdicts: Executive Summary*, MR-889-ICJ, 1997, $15.00.

Peterson, M. A., *Summary of Research Results: Trends and Patterns in Civil Jury Verdicts*, P-7222-ICJ, 1986. (Testimony before the Subcommittee on Oversight, Committee on Ways and Means, United States House of Representatives, March 1986.) $4.00.

_____ , *Civil Juries in the 1980s: Trends in Jury Trials and Verdicts in California and Cook County, Illinois*, R-3466-ICJ, 1987. $7.50.

Peterson, M. A., and G. L. Priest, *The Civil Jury: Trends in Trials and Verdicts, Cook County, Illinois, 1960-1979*, R-2881-ICJ, 1982. $7.50.

ECONOMIC EFFECTS OF THE LIABILITY SYSTEM

General

Carroll, S. J., A. Abrahamse, M. S. Marquis, and M. E. Vaiana, *Liability System Incentives to Consume Excess Medical Care*, DRU-1264-ICJ, 1995. Free.

Johnson, L. L., *Cost-Benefit Analysis and Voluntary Safety Standards for Consumer Products*, R-2882-ICJ, 1982. $7.50.

Reuter, P., *The Economic Consequences of Expanded Corporate Liability: An Exploratory Study*, N-2807-ICJ, 1988. $7.50.

Product Liability

Dunworth, T., *Product Liability and the Business Sector: Litigation Trends in Federal Courts*, R-3668-ICJ, 1988. $7.50.

Eads, G., and P. Reuter, *Designing Safer Products: Corporate Responses to Product Liability Law and Regulation*, R-3022-ICJ, 1983. $15.00.

_____ , *Designing Safer Products: Corporate Responses to Product Liability Law and Regulation*, P-7089-ICJ, 1985. (Reprinted from the *Journal of Product Liability*, Vol. 7, 1985.) $4.00.

Garber, S., *Product Liability and the Economics of Pharmaceuticals and Medical Devices*, R-4285-ICJ, 1993. $15.00.

Hensler, D. R., *Summary of Research Results on Product Liability*, P-7271-ICJ, 1986. (Statement submitted to the Committee on the Judiciary, United States Senate, October 1986.) $4.00.

_____ , *What We Know and Don't Know About Product Liability*, P-7775-ICJ, 1993. (Statement submitted to the Commerce Committee, United States Senate, September 1991.) $4.00.

Peterson, M. A., *Civil Juries in the 1980s: Trends in Jury Trials and Verdicts in California and Cook County, Illinois*, R-3466-ICJ, 1987. $7.50.

Law and the Changing American Workplace

Darling-Hammond, L., and T. J. Kniesner, *The Law and Economics of Workers' Compensation*, R-2716-ICJ, 1980. $7.50.

Dertouzos, J. N., E. Holland, and P. A. Ebener, *The Legal and Economic Consequences of Wrongful Termination*, R-3602-ICJ, 1988. $7.50.

Dertouzos, J. N., and L. A. Karoly, *Labor-Market Responses to Employer Liability*, R-3989-ICJ, 1992. $7.50.

Victor, R. B., *Workers' Compensation and Workplace Safety: The Nature of Employer Financial Incentives*, R-2979-ICJ, 1982. $7.50.

Victor, R. B., L. R. Cohen, and C. E. Phelps, *Workers' Compensation and Workplace Safety: Some Lessons from Economic Theory*, R-2918-ICJ, 1982. $7.50.

COMPENSATION SYSTEMS

System Design

Darling-Hammond, L., and T. J. Kniesner, *The Law and Economics of Workers' Compensation*, R-2716-ICJ, 1980. $7.50.

Hammitt, J. K., R. L. Houchens, S. S. Polin, and J. E. Rolph, *Automobile Accident Compensation: Volume IV, State Rules*, R-3053-ICJ, 1985. $7.50.

Hammitt, J. K., and J. E. Rolph, *Limiting Liability for Automobile Accidents: Are No-Fault Tort Thresholds Effective?* N-2418-ICJ, 1985. $4.00.

Hensler, D. R., *Resolving Mass Toxic Torts: Myths and Realities*, P-7631-ICJ, 1990. (Reprinted from the *University of Illinois Law Review*, Vol. 1989, No. 1, 1989.) $4.00.

_____ , *Assessing Claims Resolution Facilities: What We Need to Know*, RP-107, 1992. (Reprinted from *Law and Contemporary Problems*, Vol. 53, No. 4, Autumn 1990.) Free.

King, E. M., and J. P. Smith, *Computing Economic Loss in Cases of Wrongful Death*, R-3549-ICJ, 1988. $10.00.

Peterson, M. A., and M. Selvin, *Resolution of Mass Torts: Toward a Framework for Evaluation of Aggregative Procedures*, N-2805-ICJ, 1988. $7.50.

Rolph, E. S., *Framing the Compensation Inquiry*, RP-115, 1992. (Reprinted from the *Cardozo Law Review*, Vol. 13, No. 6, April 1992.) Free.

Victor, R. B., *Workers' Compensation and Workplace Safety: The Nature of Employer Financial Incentives*, R-2979-ICJ, 1982. $7.50.

Victor, R. B., L. R. Cohen, and C. E. Phelps, *Workers' Compensation and Workplace Safety: Some Lessons from Economic Theory*, R-2918-ICJ, 1982. $7.50.

Performance

Abrahamse, A., and S. J. Carroll, *The Effects of a Choice Auto Insurance Plan on Insurance Costs*, MR-540-ICJ, 1995. $13.00.

Carroll, S. J., and A. Abrahamse, *The Effects of a Proposed No-Fault Plan on the Costs of Auto Insurance in California: An Updated Analysis*, IP-146-1, January 1996. Free.

Carroll, S. J., and J. S. Kakalik, *No-Fault Approaches to Compensating Auto Accident Victims*, RP-229, 1993. (Reprinted from *The Journal of Risk and Insurance*, Vol. 60, No. 2, 1993.) Free.

Carroll, S. J., A. Abrahamse, and M. E. Vaiana, *The Costs of Excess Medical Claims for Automobile Personal Injuries*, DB-139-ICJ, 1995. $6.00.

Carroll, S. J., A. Abrahamse, M. S. Marquis, and M. E. Vaiana, *Liability System Incentives to Consume Excess Medical Care*, DRU-1264-ICJ, 1995. Free.

Carroll, S. J., J. S. Kakalik, N. M. Pace, and J. L. Adams, *No-Fault Approaches to Compensating People Injured in Automobile Accidents*, R-4019-ICJ, 1991. $20.00.

Carroll, S. J., and J. S. Kakalik, with D. Adamson, *No-Fault Automobile Insurance: A Policy Perspective*, R-4019/1-ICJ, 1991. $4.00.

Hensler, D. R., M. S. Marquis, A. Abrahamse, S. H. Berry, P. A. Ebener, E. G. Lewis, E. A. Lind, R. J. MacCoun, W. G. Manning, J. A. Rogowski, and M. E. Vaiana, *Compensation for Accidental Injuries in the United States*, R-3999-HHS/ICJ, 1991. $20.00.

_____ , *Compensation for Accidental Injuries in the United States: Executive Summary*, R-3999/1-HHS/ICJ, 1991. $4.00.

_____ , *Compensation for Accidental Injuries: Research Design and Methods*, N-3230-HHS/ICJ, 1991. $15.00.

King, E. M., and J. P. Smith, *Economic Loss and Compensation in Aviation Accidents*, R-3551-ICJ, 1988. $10.00.

O'Connell, J., S. J. Carroll, M. Horowitz, and A. Abrahamse, *Consumer Choice in the Auto Insurance Market*, RP-254, 1994. (Reprinted from the *Maryland Law Review*, Vol. 52, 1993.) Free.

O'Connell, J., S. J. Carroll, M. Horowitz, A. Abrahamse, and D. Kaiser, *The Costs of Consumer Choice for Auto Insurance in States Without No-Fault Insurance*, RP-442, 1995. (Reprinted from *Maryland Law Review*, Vol. 54, No. 2, 1995.) Free.

Peterson, M. A., *Giving Away Money: Comparative Comments on Claims Resolution Facilities*, RP-108, 1992. (Reprinted from *Law and Contemporary Problems*, Vol. 53, No. 4, Autumn 1990.) Free.

Peterson, M. A., and M. Selvin, *Mass Justice: The Limited and Unlimited Power of Courts*, RP-116, 1992. (Reprinted from *Law and Contemporary Problems*, Vol. 54, No. 3, Summer 1991.) Free.

Rolph, J. E., with J. K. Hammitt, R. L. Houchens, and S. S. Polin, *Automobile Accident Compensation: Volume I, Who Pays How Much How Soon?* R-3050-ICJ, 1985. $4.00.

SPECIAL STUDIES

Hensler, D. R., and M. E. Reddy, *California Lawyers View the Future: A Report to the Commission on the Future of the Legal Profession and the State Bar*, MR-528-ICJ, 1994. $13.00.

Merz, J. F., and N. M. Pace, *Trends in Patent Litigation: The Apparent Influence of Strengthened Patents Attributable to the Court of Appeals for the Federal Circuit*, RP-426, 1995. (Reprinted from *Journal of the Patent and Trademark Office Society*, Vol. 76, No. 8, August 1994.) Free.

An annotated bibliography, CP-253 (12/96), provides a list of RAND publications in the civil justice area through 1996 To request the bibliography or to obtain more information about the Institute for Civil Justice, please write the Institute at this address: The Institute for Civil Justice, RAND, 1700 Main Street, P.O. Box 2138, Santa Monica, California 90407-2138, or call (310) 393-0411, x6916.